The History of Amsterdam

Crafted by Skriuwer

Copyright © 2024 by Skriuwer.

All rights reserved. No part of this book may be used or reproduced in any form whatsoever without written permission except in the case of brief quotations in critical articles or reviews.

For more information, contact : **kontakt@skriuwer.com** (www.skriuwer.com)

Table of Contents

Chapter 1: Origins of Amsterdam

- 1.1 Early Settlements
- 1.2 The Building of the Dam
- 1.3 Amsterdam's First Charter
- 1.4 The Role of Trade in Early Growth
- 1.5 Religious and Political Climate

Chapter 2: The Golden Age of Amsterdam

- 2.1 Rise of the Dutch East India Company
- 2.2 Amsterdam as a Financial Center
- 2.3 Cultural Flourishing
- 2.4 Architectural Expansion
- 2.5 Social and Economic Inequality

Chapter 3: Amsterdam in the 18th Century

- 3.1 The Decline of Dutch Power
- 3.2 The French Occupation
- 3.3 Economic and Social Changes
- 3.4 The Impact of Enlightenment Ideas
- 3.5 Urban Development and Population Growth

Chapter 4: The 19th Century and Industrialization

- 4.1 The Kingdom of the Netherlands
- 4.2 Industrialization and Economic Change
- 4.3 Social Reform Movements
- 4.4 Urbanization and Housing
- 4.5 Cultural and Artistic Renaissance

Chapter 5: Amsterdam and World War I

- 5.1 The Netherlands' Neutrality
- 5.2 Economic Impact of the War
- 5.3 Social Tensions and Strikes
- 5.4 The Post-War Recovery
- 5.5 The Rise of Modern Amsterdam

Chapter 6: Amsterdam during World War II

- 6.1 The German Occupation
- 6.2 The Jewish Community and the Holocaust
- 6.3 Resistance and Collaboration
- 6.4 The Hunger Winter
- 6.5 Liberation and Aftermath

Chapter 7: Post-War Reconstruction and Growth

- 7.1 The Marshall Plan and Economic Recovery
- 7.2 The Housing Crisis and New Urban Development
- 7.3 Social Change and the Welfare State
- 7.4 The Rise of Tourism
- 7.5 Cultural Renaissance

Chapter 8: The 1960s and 1970s - A Time of Change

- 8.1 The Provo Movement
- 8.2 Social Reforms and Civil Rights
- 8.3 Drug Culture and Policy
- 8.4 The Women's Movement
- 8.5 Economic Challenges and Innovation

Chapter 9: Amsterdam in the 1980s and 1990s

- 9.1 Economic Liberalization
- 9.2 The Housing Market Boom
- 9.3 Immigration and Multiculturalism
- 9.4 The Growth of the Service Sector
- 9.5 Cultural and Artistic Developments

Chapter 10: The New Millennium

- 10.1 Amsterdam in a Globalized World
- 10.2 Sustainability and Urban Planning
- 10.3 Technological Innovation
- 10.4 Social Policy and Inclusion
- 10.5 The Future of Amsterdam

Chapter 11: Amsterdam's Architectural Heritage

- 11.1 Medieval and Renaissance Architecture
- 11.2 The Canal Ring
- 11.3 Art Deco and Modernism
- 11.4 Post-War Architecture
- 11.5 Contemporary Architecture

Chapter 12: Amsterdam's Cultural Influence

- 12.1 The Dutch Masters and Amsterdam
- 12.2 The Role of Amsterdam in Literature
- 12.3 Music and Performing Arts
- 12.4 Museums and Cultural Institutions
- 12.5 Festivals and Public Celebrations

Chapter 13: Amsterdam's Role in Dutch Politics

- 13.1 The Formation of the Dutch Republic
- 13.2 Amsterdam and the Dutch Monarchy
- 13.3 The Influence of Amsterdam on National Policy
- 13.4 Amsterdam as a Capital City
- 13.5 Major Political Movements in Amsterdam

Chapter 14: Amsterdam in International Relations

- 14.1 Amsterdam's Role in the European Union
- 14.2 Amsterdam and Global Trade
- 14.3 Diplomatic Presence in Amsterdam
- 14.4 The Impact of International Organizations
- 14.5 Amsterdam's Role in Global Environmental Initiatives

Chapter 15: Conclusion and Reflections

- 15.1 Summary of Amsterdam's Historical Development
- 15.2 The Enduring Legacy of Amsterdam
- 15.3 Lessons from Amsterdam's History
- 15.4 Amsterdam's Global Influence
- 15.5 The Future of Amsterdam

Chapter 1

Origins of Amsterdam

Early Settlements

The origins of Amsterdam can be traced back to a convergence of geography, natural resources, and the adaptability of its early inhabitants. The Amstel River, which flows through the heart of what is now a bustling metropolis, served as the lifeblood for these nascent communities. The river not only provided a source of water but also facilitated trade and communication, which were critical for the survival and growth of early settlements.

Archaeological evidence suggests that the first human activity in the Amsterdam area dates back to the Mesolithic period, around 5000 BC, when small groups of hunter-gatherers roamed the lush, marshy landscape. These early inhabitants relied on the abundant natural resources of the region, including fish from the river and game from the surrounding woodlands. As these communities gradually transitioned to more settled lifestyles, they began to exploit the fertile land for agriculture, establishing the foundations for more permanent settlements.

By the 12th century, the inhabitants of the Amstel region had formed small fishing villages. The strategic location of the Amstel River made it a vital artery for trade. As commerce flourished, the small settlements began to grow, drawing in settlers from surrounding areas attracted by the economic opportunities. This convergence of population and trade was instrumental in the development of what would eventually become Amsterdam.

The construction of a dam in the Amstel River marked a significant turning point in the region's early history. In the late 12th century, local inhabitants erected a dam to control the river's flow and to provide a safe haven from flooding. This structure not only protected the settlements but also created a more stable environment conducive to trade and agriculture. The name "Amsterdam" itself is derived from this dam, with "Amstel" referring to the river and "dam" denoting the constructed barrier. This innovation laid the groundwork for urban development, as the dam became the focal point around which the community could expand.

As trade routes expanded, Amsterdam's strategic location became increasingly advantageous. The establishment of merchant networks allowed for the exchange of goods, ideas, and cultures. The river facilitated the transportation of goods to and from the North Sea, connecting

Amsterdam to broader European markets. This flourishing trade environment attracted artisans, merchants, and laborers, contributing to the burgeoning population of the area.

In 1300, Amsterdam received its first charter, granting it official city rights. This milestone was a testament to the success of its early settlements and the significant role of the Amstel River in shaping the city's identity. The charter allowed for greater self-governance, which further encouraged trade and migration, solidifying Amsterdam's position as a vital economic hub in the region.

The early religious and political climate also played a crucial role in the formation of these communities. The settlement around the Amstel River was characterized by a mix of religious beliefs, with Christianity slowly becoming the dominant faith in the area. Local governance structures began to emerge, with councils formed to address the needs and challenges of the growing population.

In summary, the early settlements along the Amstel River were a product of environmental advantages, strategic trade opportunities, and the adaptability of its inhabitants. These initial communities laid the foundation for Amsterdam's transformation into a thriving city, with the Amstel River serving as both a literal and metaphorical artery of growth and development. The interplay of commerce, governance, and culture in these formative years would set the stage for Amsterdam's evolution into one of the most significant cities in Europe.

The Building of the Dam

The origins of Amsterdam are intricately tied to the construction of a dam on the Amstel River, a pivotal event that not only gave the city its name but also laid the foundation for its early development and prosperity. In the late 12th century, the area that would become Amsterdam was characterized by a series of small settlements along the banks of the Amstel River, primarily inhabited by fishermen and farmers. The river itself was a critical waterway, providing access to trade routes and facilitating commerce with neighboring regions.

As settlements grew, the need for managing water became increasingly apparent. The region was prone to flooding, and the locals understood that controlling the river's flow was essential for their survival and economic stability. In response to these challenges, the inhabitants initiated the construction of a dam in the Amstel River around the year 1270. This dam served multiple purposes: it controlled the river's water levels, protected the surrounding lands from flooding, and created a navigable harbor for boats and ships.

The dam-building project marked a significant turning point for the nascent community. It allowed for the establishment of a more structured and organized settlement, which would eventually evolve into a thriving urban center. As the dam was completed, the settlement began to attract merchants and traders, who were drawn to the economic opportunities presented by the newly protected harbor. This influx of commerce and trade laid the groundwork for what would become Amsterdam's reputation as a key trading hub in northern Europe.

The name "Amsterdam" itself is derived from this landmark event. The term "Amstel" references the river, while "dam" signifies the dam constructed across it. Thus, the very identity of the city is rooted in this essential infrastructure project, symbolizing the interplay between nature and human ingenuity that characterized its early development.

Moreover, the construction of the dam facilitated the creation of a marketplace, which became a focal point for trade and social interaction. As merchants set up their stalls, the area began to flourish, and by the late 13th century, Amsterdam was granted its first charter, marking its recognition as a city. This charter was a crucial milestone, as it conferred certain rights and privileges to the inhabitants, including the ability to govern themselves, collect taxes, and establish laws. The dam had not only shaped the geography of the region but also catalyzed the political and social evolution of what was to become one of the most influential cities in the world.

The dam's construction also had long-term implications for the urban planning and architectural development of Amsterdam. The layout of the city gradually evolved around this central dam, leading to the establishment of streets and canals that would define its unique urban landscape. The canals, in particular, became instrumental in facilitating trade and transportation, allowing Amsterdam to grow and expand its reach in the commercial world.

In summary, the building of the dam on the Amstel River was a defining moment in the early history of Amsterdam. It provided the physical and economic infrastructure necessary for the settlement to flourish, established the city's identity, and set the stage for its transformation into a vibrant hub of trade, culture, and innovation. The dam not only shaped the landscape but also fostered a sense of community and identity among its inhabitants, a legacy that continues to resonate in Amsterdam's cultural and historical narrative today.

Amsterdam's First Charter

Amsterdam's journey toward becoming a recognized city began with its acquisition of city rights in 1300, a pivotal moment that marked the transition from a modest settlement to a significant urban center. This chapter in Amsterdam's history encapsulates the socio-political context of the time, the motivations behind the granting of city rights, and the implications for the city's development.

In the late 13th century, Amsterdam was primarily a fishing village situated along the Amstel River, characterized by its strategic location that facilitated trade. The settlement's growth was already evident, spurred on by the burgeoning commerce that emerged from its advantageous position near major trade routes. However, despite this growth, Amsterdam lacked formal recognition and the autonomy that came with city status. This lack of status hindered its ability to govern itself and fully harness its economic potential.

The demand for city rights was influenced by broader trends across Europe, where many growing settlements sought similar recognition to enhance their administration, security, and economic opportunities. The granting of city rights typically included privileges such as the ability to hold markets, establish local governance, and impose taxes. These rights were not merely ceremonial but were essential for the economic and political empowerment of the settlement.

In 1300, the opportunity arose when the count of Holland, Floris V, recognized the potential of Amsterdam as a burgeoning trade hub. The count's motivations were twofold: to strengthen his control over the region and to encourage the growth of commerce that would bolster his own power. By granting Amsterdam city rights, he effectively endorsed its importance within his territory and the wider European trade networks. This strategic move allowed Floris to consolidate his influence over a key economic player and to promote stability in the region.

The official charter, known as the "Stadsrechten," endowed Amsterdam with various privileges. It allowed the city to establish its own laws and governance structures, which began with the formation of a city council. This council was crucial for the implementation of local laws and for maintaining order, thus fostering a sense of community and civic responsibility among its inhabitants. The charter also facilitated the establishment of a marketplace, which was vital for trade and commerce, allowing merchants to gather, exchange goods, and conduct business under the protection of the city.

Moreover, the acquisition of city rights had profound implications for Amsterdam's social fabric. As a recognized city, it became an attractive destination for migrants seeking economic opportunities, contributing to a growing, diverse population. This influx of people not only enhanced the labor force but also enriched the cultural landscape of Amsterdam, laying the groundwork for its future as a cosmopolitan center.

The granting of city rights also marked the beginning of a more structured relationship between the city and its surrounding regions. As Amsterdam began to prosper, it became a hub for trade and commerce, attracting merchants from across Europe. The city's economy flourished, leading to the establishment of guilds and a burgeoning merchant class that would play a crucial role in its development.

In conclusion, Amsterdam's acquisition of city rights in 1300 was a transformative moment in its history. It provided the foundation for political autonomy, economic expansion, and social development, setting the stage for the city's emergence as a significant player in regional and international trade. The charter not only legitimized Amsterdam's aspirations but also catalyzed its evolution into one of Europe's most important cities, paving the way for the Golden Age that would follow in the 17th century.

The Role of Trade in Early Growth

The early history of Amsterdam is intricately linked to its strategic location along the Amstel River, which served as a vital conduit for trade and commerce. Emerging around the 12th century, the settlement's growth was primarily fueled by its advantageous position that allowed for the seamless movement of goods between the interior of the Netherlands and the North Sea. This geographical advantage laid the groundwork for what would become a bustling hub of trade.

Initially, Amsterdam's economy was rooted in agriculture and fishing, with local farmers and fishermen utilizing the river's resources. However, as the settlement began to grow, it quickly transformed into a trading post, capitalizing on the increasing demand for goods such as grain, fish, and timber. The establishment of the dam across the Amstel River not only provided protection against flooding but also facilitated the collection of tolls from passing ships, generating early revenue for the burgeoning community. This damming effort, which is reflected in the city's name, was instrumental in establishing Amsterdam as a key economic player in the region.

During the late Middle Ages, Amsterdam's trade network expanded significantly. The city became a focal point for merchants from various regions, including the Hanseatic League, a powerful alliance of trading cities in Northern Europe. These connections allowed Amsterdam to import a wide variety of goods, including cloth, spices, and luxury items from distant lands. As trade flourished, so too did the population, which attracted a diverse array of residents, including merchants, craftsmen, and laborers, all drawn by the economic opportunities the city offered.

The late 13th and early 14th centuries marked a pivotal period in Amsterdam's trading history when the city was granted its first charter in 1300. This charter granted Amsterdam the rights to hold markets, thereby formalizing its status as a commercial center. The establishment of regular markets drew merchants from across Europe, which in turn stimulated local production and craftsmanship. The increased volume of trade not only bolstered the economy but also cultivated a vibrant urban culture centered around commerce.

The growth of trade also had significant implications for the city's infrastructure. As the demand for goods increased, so did the need for improved transport and storage facilities. The construction of warehouses along the canals, which would later become iconic features of the city, allowed merchants to store goods securely. The extensive canal network, developed in the 17th century, further enhanced Amsterdam's role as a major port city, allowing for the efficient movement of cargo and access to international markets.

Moreover, the rise of trade led to the formation of guilds, which were associations of merchants and artisans that regulated the economy and maintained quality standards. These guilds played a crucial role in protecting the interests of their members, establishing fair practices, and fostering cooperation among businesses. They also contributed to the social fabric of the city, creating a sense of community among traders and craftsmen.

As trade continued to flourish, it laid the foundation for the emergence of financial institutions in Amsterdam. The need for credit and investment in maritime trade led to the development of banking services, ultimately transforming the city into a financial center. The establishment of the Amsterdam Stock Exchange in the early 17th century marked a significant milestone, enabling the mobilization of capital for trade ventures and further consolidating the city's status as a global trading powerhouse.

In conclusion, trade was the lifeblood of early Amsterdam, shaping its economic structure, urban landscape, and social dynamics. The strategic location along the Amstel River, coupled with the entrepreneurial spirit of its inhabitants, spurred Amsterdam's growth into one of the most important trading cities in Europe by the late Middle Ages. This early foundation of commerce not only established the city as a commercial hub but also set the stage for its remarkable evolution through subsequent centuries.

Religious and Political Climate

In the early history of Amsterdam, the interplay of religious and political dynamics significantly shaped the city's development. Situated along the Amstel River, Amsterdam began as a small fishing village in the late 12th century, but it quickly transformed into a burgeoning town due, in part, to the influences of religion and governance.

Initially, Amsterdam was part of the Catholic Church's influence in the Low Countries, as were much of Europe. The Catholic Church played a central role in the daily lives of the inhabitants, guiding moral conduct and community activities. The establishment of the first church, dedicated to Saint Nicholas, marked the importance of Christianity in the town's identity. This church not only served as a religious center but also as a social hub, where community members gathered for festivals, fairs, and other communal events. The church's authority was pivotal in maintaining social order and providing education, thus facilitating the growth of early settlements.

However, the religious landscape began to shift dramatically in the 16th century, coinciding with the rise of Protestantism during the Reformation. The movement gained traction in the Netherlands, leading to significant social and political upheaval. Amsterdam, which had originally been a Catholic stronghold, became a refuge for Protestants fleeing persecution in other parts of Europe, particularly France and the Southern Netherlands. This influx of religious dissidents contributed to a more diverse population and helped to lay the groundwork for the city's future as a center of tolerance.

The political climate of the time was also marked by the struggle for independence from Spanish rule. The Eighty Years' War (1568-1648) catalyzed the desire for self-governance and religious freedom. Amsterdam's leaders, known as the regents, began to assert their power and autonomy, leading to the establishment of a municipal government that could represent the interests of its citizens. This shift not only empowered local governance but also facilitated the development of a unique political identity that emphasized civic freedom and individual rights, values that would later come to define Amsterdam.

As the city gained its first charter in 1300, granting it the rights of a city, the political landscape continued to evolve. The charter allowed for a degree of self-governance, enabling the inhabitants to elect their own officials and manage local affairs. This burgeoning sense of democracy distinguished Amsterdam from other European cities that were still under feudal or monarchical control. The political structure that emerged was characterized by a blend of oligarchic rule and civic participation, allowing for a relatively progressive governance model for its time.

The mixture of religious tolerance and political innovation positioned Amsterdam as a haven for diverse populations, leading to a flourishing of ideas and commerce. The city became known for its acceptance of different faiths, including Judaism, which found a significant community in Amsterdam after the expulsion from Spain and Portugal. This religious diversity attracted merchants, intellectuals, and artists, further stimulating the economic and cultural growth of the city.

In summary, the religious and political climate of early Amsterdam was instrumental in shaping the city's identity and trajectory. The transition from a Catholic stronghold to a center of Protestantism and religious tolerance, coupled with the evolution of local governance, established Amsterdam as a vibrant and dynamic urban center. These factors not only spurred economic growth but also laid the foundation for the city's enduring legacy as a place of refuge, innovation, and cultural richness. The early embrace of diversity and self-governance would continue to influence Amsterdam's development well into the modern era, making it a model of coexistence and civic engagement in an increasingly interconnected world.

Chapter 2

The Golden Age of Amsterdam

Rise of the Dutch East India Company

The establishment of the Dutch East India Company, or Vereenigde Oostindische Compagnie (VOC), in 1602 marked a watershed moment in Amsterdam's history, fundamentally altering its economic landscape and solidifying its status as a global trading hub. The VOC was not only the first multinational corporation in history but also a pioneering entity in the world of international trade, significantly contributing to the wealth and global influence of Amsterdam during the 17th century, a period often referred to as the Dutch Golden Age.

In the context of an expanding European interest in Asian trade, the VOC was formed to consolidate various trading ventures under a single banner, allowing for more efficient management and stronger bargaining power against competitors. The company was granted a monopoly on Dutch trade in the East Indies, enabling it to control the lucrative spice trade, among other goods such as silk, tea, and porcelain. This monopoly was a double-edged sword; while it allowed for unprecedented profits, it also necessitated military and naval strength to protect trade routes and interests, leading to conflicts with indigenous powers and European rivals, notably Portugal and England.

Amsterdam served as the principal base of operations for the VOC, with its canals and port facilities perfectly suited to accommodate the influx of ships laden with exotic goods. The wealth generated by the VOC flowed into the city, fueling an economic boom that stimulated various sectors. The influx of capital led to investments in infrastructure, commerce, and the arts, creating a vibrant cultural atmosphere that attracted artists, intellectuals, and merchants from across Europe. The VOC's activities also fostered a burgeoning financial market in Amsterdam; shares of the company were traded on the Amsterdam Stock Exchange, which became the world's first stock market.

The company's global reach extended far beyond trade; it played a crucial role in establishing the Dutch colonial empire. The VOC facilitated the establishment of numerous settlements and trading posts in Asia, including Batavia (modern-day Jakarta), Ceylon (Sri Lanka), and parts of India. These outposts not only served as commercial hubs but also as strategic military bases, allowing the VOC to dominate trade routes and expand Dutch influence. The wealth generated

14

from these colonies further enriched Amsterdam, reinforcing its position as a center of global trade.

However, the VOC was not without its challenges. The company faced escalating competition from other European powers and internal mismanagement. By the late 17th century, the initial profits began to dwindle, leading to financial difficulties. Despite these challenges, the VOC left an indelible mark on Amsterdam and the Netherlands as a whole. Its legacy is evident in the city's architecture, with grand merchant houses lining the canals, built with the wealth accumulated from trade.

In summary, the rise of the Dutch East India Company was pivotal to Amsterdam's wealth and global influence during the 17th century. It transformed the city into a bustling center of trade and finance, fostering an environment ripe for cultural flourishing. The VOC's impact extended beyond economic realms, shaping the very identity of Amsterdam as a cosmopolitan city intertwined with the global flow of goods and ideas. The success and eventual decline of the VOC also serve as a reminder of the complexities and challenges inherent in global commerce, a narrative that continues to resonate in today's interconnected world.

Amsterdam as a Financial Center

In the 17th century, Amsterdam emerged as the world's leading financial hub, a transformation driven by a confluence of historical, economic, and social factors. This period, often referred to as the Dutch Golden Age, saw the city flourish as a center of trade, finance, and innovation, establishing it as a model for modern financial systems.

One of the primary catalysts for Amsterdam's ascendance in global finance was the establishment of the Dutch East India Company (VOC) in 1602. The VOC was the first multinational corporation in history, and it fundamentally altered how trade was conducted. By issuing shares and allowing individuals to invest in maritime expeditions, the company democratized investment, paving the way for a stock market that was accessible to a broader segment of the population. Amsterdam's stock exchange, founded in 1608, became the first official stock exchange, where shares of the VOC and other companies were traded. This innovation allowed for the pooling of capital, which was essential for financing the ambitious and risky voyages that drove the Dutch mercantile empire.

As the VOC expanded its reach across Asia, it established trade routes that brought spices, silks, and other exotic goods to Europe. The wealth generated by this trade not only enriched the company but also the city of Amsterdam itself. With profits flowing in, a burgeoning merchant class emerged, further stimulating economic activity. The influx of wealth allowed for investment in infrastructure, public works, and the arts, enhancing the city's appeal as a financial center.

The financial innovations of the period were not limited to trade; they also encompassed banking practices. Amsterdam became home to pioneering banking institutions such as the Bank of Amsterdam, established in 1609. This bank introduced a stable currency and a system of deposits that facilitated trade. It operated on a model of sound banking principles, providing the security that merchants required for their transactions. The Bank of Amsterdam's reputation for reliability attracted foreign traders and investors, solidifying the city's role as a financial nexus.

Moreover, Amsterdam's geographical location was advantageous. Situated at the intersection of key European trade routes and with access to the North Sea, it became an essential port for merchants from across the continent. This strategic position allowed Amsterdam to serve not only as a hub for the import and export of goods but also as a center for the exchange of financial instruments. The city's merchants and bankers developed a sophisticated understanding of risk management and investment strategies, further enhancing its status in the global marketplace.

The 17th century also witnessed significant social and political changes that contributed to Amsterdam's financial prominence. The relative religious tolerance and political stability in the Dutch Republic attracted a diverse population of merchants, traders, and financiers. This multicultural milieu fostered an environment ripe for innovation and collaboration, allowing new financial ideas and practices to flourish.

However, the rise of Amsterdam as a financial center was not without challenges. The city faced competition from other emerging financial hubs, particularly London and Paris. The eventual decline of the VOC and the challenges posed by wars in the late 17th century would eventually lead to a shift in financial power. Nevertheless, the foundation laid during this golden period in Amsterdam's history would have lasting impacts on global finance.

In summary, Amsterdam's rise as a financial center in the 17th century can be attributed to its pioneering financial institutions, innovative trading practices, strategic geographical position, and a culture of tolerance and entrepreneurship. The legacy of this period endures, influencing modern financial systems and practices worldwide.

Cultural Flourishing in Amsterdam

The 17th century, often referred to as the Dutch Golden Age, marked a period of extraordinary cultural flourishing in Amsterdam, characterized by remarkable advancements in art, science, and intellectual thought. This era saw the rise of iconic artists and thinkers who not only shaped the cultural landscape of the Netherlands but left an indelible mark on Western civilization.

Artistic Achievements

At the heart of this cultural renaissance were the visual arts, with Amsterdam emerging as a hub for painters whose works continue to resonate with audiences worldwide. Among the most notable figures of this period was Rembrandt van Rijn, whose innovative use of light and shadow, known as chiaroscuro, revolutionized portrait painting. Rembrandt's ability to capture the human condition in all its complexity is epitomized in masterpieces such as The Night Watch and The Anatomy Lesson of Dr. Nicolaes Tulp. His work reflects not only technical prowess but also deep psychological insight, making his portraits dynamic and lifelike.

Another luminary of this period was Johannes Vermeer, celebrated for his exquisite use of color and light. Vermeer's intimate depictions of domestic life, such as Girl with a Pearl Earring and The Milkmaid, invite viewers into the quiet moments of 17th-century Dutch society. His meticulous attention to detail and innovative compositions have earned him a revered place in the canon of art history. The paintings of both Rembrandt and Vermeer highlight the era's emphasis on realism and the exploration of everyday life, setting a new standard for artistic expression.

The Science and Intellectual Landscape

While the visual arts flourished, Amsterdam was also a center for scientific inquiry and intellectual advancement. The period saw the establishment of institutions such as the University of Amsterdam, which became a beacon for scholars and scientists. The Enlightenment ideas that permeated Europe found fertile ground in Amsterdam, fostering an environment where intellectual discourse thrived.

Figures like Baruch Spinoza, a philosopher whose ideas on ethics and the nature of reality challenged traditional religious views, emerged from this vibrant intellectual milieu. Spinoza's work laid the foundation for modern philosophy, emphasizing reason and empirical observation, which mirrored the scientific advancements of the time.

The Role of the Dutch East India Company

The economic prosperity brought about by the Dutch East India Company (VOC) also played a significant role in the cultural flourishing of Amsterdam. As the VOC established trade routes across Asia and beyond, the influx of wealth and exotic goods stimulated artistic patronage. Wealthy merchants commissioned artworks and funded cultural institutions, creating a demand for artistic output that fueled the careers of many artists.

The VOC's success not only enriched individual lives but also contributed to a collective cultural identity in Amsterdam. The city became a cosmopolitan center, where diverse influences converged, enriching the local culture and inspiring a sense of pride in Dutch heritage.

Social Commentary and Cultural Reflection

The art and literature of the time often reflected the complexities of Dutch society, including themes of social stratification and the moral dilemmas of wealth. The emergence of genre painting, depicting scenes of daily life, allowed artists to comment on the social realities of their time. This genre, exemplified by the works of painters like Jan Steen, provided a lens through which viewers could engage with contemporary issues, from the pleasures and pitfalls of bourgeois life to the moral lessons of excess and virtue.

In summary, the Golden Age of Amsterdam was a remarkable period of cultural flourishing that produced some of history's most celebrated artists and thinkers. The synergy between economic prosperity, artistic innovation, and intellectual inquiry created a vibrant cultural tapestry that not only defined the era but continues to influence art and philosophy today. The legacy of this period remains a defining characteristic of Amsterdam, shaping its identity as a center of culture, creativity, and enlightenment.

Architectural Expansion

The 17th century, often referred to as the Golden Age of Amsterdam, was not only a period of profound economic prosperity and cultural flourishing but also a transformative era for the city's architectural landscape. Central to this transformation was the development of Amsterdam's iconic canal system and the distinctive merchant houses that lined these waterways, which have become emblematic of the city's identity.

The origins of Amsterdam's canals can be traced back to the necessity of managing the region's waterlogged terrain. The city lies in a delta region, where the Amstel River and various waterways posed both a challenge and an opportunity. In the early 17th century, urban planners embarked on an ambitious project to construct a series of concentric canals, which were designed not only for drainage and flood prevention but also to facilitate transportation and commerce. This canal system included the Herengracht, Prinsengracht, and Keizersgracht, among others, and was ingeniously designed to optimize trade routes while providing an elegant urban aesthetic.

The creation of the canals was a monumental engineering feat that utilized innovative techniques for water management. This included the construction of locks and sluices, which allowed for control of water levels and the safe passage of ships. The canals were lined with trees and provided ample space for streets, fostering a sense of community and enhancing the city's livability. By 1650, Amsterdam had developed a sophisticated network of canals that not only served functional purposes but also symbolized the city's wealth and status as a major trading hub.

The architectural style of the merchant houses that emerged during this period reflected the immense wealth generated by trade and commerce. Built primarily by wealthy merchants, these houses were characterized by their narrow facades, gabled roofs, and ornate decorations. The typical merchant house was designed to maximize space, often extending deep into the block while remaining narrow at the street front. This design was not only practical but also showcased the affluence of the owners.

The use of bricks, which were widely available due to the flourishing brick-making industry, allowed for elaborate decorative elements. Gables were often adorned with intricate carvings and sculptures, and many houses featured large windows that let in abundant natural light, a luxury at the time. The iconic 'trap door' or hoisting beam at the top of the façade was a practical addition, allowing goods to be lifted directly into the upper levels, reflecting the commercial nature of these residences.

The architectural expansion during this period was not merely about aesthetics; it was also a reflection of the social hierarchy and the mercantile culture that defined Amsterdam. The wealthiest merchants lived along the most prominent canals, while the less affluent resided in the inner canals or on the outskirts. This physical manifestation of wealth created a distinctive urban landscape that is now recognized as one of the most beautiful in the world.

While the canals and merchant houses were a symbol of prosperity, they also played a significant role in shaping the social fabric of Amsterdam. The waterways served as communal spaces for trade and social interaction, fostering a sense of community among the diverse inhabitants of the city. As such, the architectural expansion of Amsterdam during its Golden Age not only transformed its skyline but also laid the groundwork for a vibrant urban culture that continues to thrive.

Today, the canals of Amsterdam are recognized as a UNESCO World Heritage site, celebrating their historical significance and the architectural ingenuity that characterized this remarkable period in the city's history. The legacy of these developments endures, as they continue to draw millions of visitors each year, fascinated by the beauty and history embedded in Amsterdam's iconic waterways and merchant houses.

Social and Economic Inequality

The Golden Age of Amsterdam, spanning the 17th century, is often celebrated for its extraordinary economic and cultural flourishing. However, amidst the backdrop of prosperity, stark social and economic inequalities became increasingly pronounced. This period saw the rise of a wealthy merchant class, primarily composed of traders and shipowners who reaped immense profits from international trade, particularly through the activities of the Dutch East India Company (VOC). At the same time, a significant portion of the population faced dire economic conditions, leading to a complex social landscape marked by contrasts between affluence and poverty.

The VOC, established in 1602, played a pivotal role in shaping Amsterdam's wealth. It monopolized trade routes to Asia, importing spices, textiles, and other valuable goods that transformed the city into a global trading hub. The influx of wealth allowed for the construction of opulent merchant houses, the commissioning of grand artworks, and the establishment of cultural institutions. The city's elite, who benefited from this booming trade, indulged in lavish lifestyles characterized by luxury and excess. Their newfound affluence manifested in a flourishing art scene, with renowned painters like Rembrandt and Vermeer capturing the lives of the wealthy, showcasing their possessions, and highlighting the stark divide between their comforts and the struggles of the lower classes.

In stark contrast, the lower classes—comprising laborers, dockworkers, and the urban poor—faced challenging living conditions. Many of these individuals were engaged in low-wage labor, often working long hours under harsh conditions. The rapid urbanization that accompanied commercial growth resulted in overcrowded and unsanitary housing. The burgeoning population of Amsterdam led to a housing crisis, with the poorest citizens relegated to cramped conditions in the city's back alleys and less desirable neighborhoods. The disparity in living conditions was evident; while the wealthy resided in spacious canal houses adorned with fine art, the impoverished lived in squalor, struggling to secure basic necessities.

Moreover, the social hierarchy in Amsterdam was not solely determined by wealth but was also intertwined with factors such as religion and ethnicity. The Protestant Reformation had left a significant mark on the city, leading to tensions between the predominantly Protestant merchant class and Catholic populations. This division often translated into economic disparities, as Catholics faced restrictions in certain professions and were often excluded from the burgeoning commercial opportunities available to their Protestant counterparts. Additionally, the Jewish community, which contributed to the city's economic activities, also experienced discrimination and marginalization despite their significant roles in trade and finance.

The social inequality of the time was further exacerbated by systemic issues such as limited access to education and healthcare for the lower classes. While the wealthy could afford private tutors and medical care, the poor relied on charity and public assistance, which were often insufficient to meet their needs. This lack of social support perpetuated cycles of poverty and limited upward mobility for the working classes.

Nevertheless, the stark contrasts between wealth and poverty during Amsterdam's Golden Age did not go unnoticed. The growing awareness of these inequalities led to discussions about social responsibility and charity among the affluent. Some wealthy citizens began to engage in philanthropic endeavors, establishing almshouses and charitable organizations aimed at alleviating the suffering of the poor. However, these efforts often fell short of addressing the root causes of inequality, indicating the persistent divide that characterized Amsterdam during this remarkable, yet complex, period of its history.

In summary, while the Golden Age of Amsterdam was marked by unparalleled economic success and cultural achievements, it also highlighted significant social and economic inequalities. The disparities in wealth and living conditions between the affluent merchant class and the struggling lower classes served as a reminder of the intricate social dynamics that defined this era, shaping the future of the city and its inhabitants.

Chapter 3

Amsterdam in the 18th Century

The Decline of Dutch Power

The 18th century marked a significant turning point for Amsterdam and the Dutch Republic, as the city began to experience a decline in power that would set the stage for its future challenges. This decline was influenced by a confluence of wars, economic downturns, and changing global dynamics that diminished Amsterdam's status as a leading trade and financial center.

During the late 17th century, the Dutch Republic, and by extension Amsterdam, reached the zenith of its power, primarily through its formidable naval prowess and expansive trade networks established by the Dutch East India Company (VOC). However, the following century brought a series of conflicts that severely strained the Republic's resources. The War of the Spanish Succession (1701-1714) was particularly detrimental, as it pitted the Dutch Republic against a coalition of powerful European nations, leading to costly military expenditures and a depletion of manpower. The prolonged nature of these conflicts drained the Dutch treasury and created internal dissent, undermining Amsterdam's economic stability.

Additionally, the rise of rival maritime powers, particularly Great Britain and France, further contributed to the decline of Dutch dominance. The British Navy's increasing control over trade routes and colonies eroded the VOC's monopoly on the spice trade, which had been a cornerstone of Amsterdam's wealth. As British and French mercantile interests expanded, Amsterdam found itself losing its competitive edge in global trade. This shift not only impacted the city's economy but also altered its demographic landscape as merchants and traders sought opportunities elsewhere.

Economic downturns in the early to mid-18th century compounded these challenges. The previously thriving trade routes became less lucrative, leading to a gradual decline in maritime commerce. The city experienced a significant decrease in shipbuilding and a corresponding rise in unemployment among sailors and dockworkers, which created a ripple effect of social unrest. The financial crisis of the late 1720s, marked by the collapse of several banks and businesses, further exacerbated the economic malaise. As the once-busy wharves and canals of Amsterdam became quieter, the city's vibrancy began to wane.

Religious and political factors also played a role in the decline of Amsterdam's prominence. The internal strife between the oligarchic regents and the rising populace led to political instability and fragmentation. The lack of a unified political strategy to address the economic and military challenges left Amsterdam vulnerable. Furthermore, the Enlightenment ideas that flourished during this period began to question traditional power structures, leading to calls for reform and greater social equity. This rising sentiment among the populace often clashed with the interests of the established elites, creating a politically charged atmosphere that detracted from collective efforts to revitalize the economy.

The culmination of these factors led to a perception of Amsterdam as a fading power in the European landscape. The once-great city, revered for its commerce and innovation, found itself grappling with the realities of a changing world order. The decline was not abrupt but gradual, reflecting the complexities of economic, military, and social transformations that characterized the 18th century.

In summary, the decline of Dutch power during the 18th century was a multifaceted phenomenon influenced by wars, economic downturns, and internal strife. As Amsterdam navigated these turbulent waters, it struggled to maintain its status as a preeminent center of trade and finance, setting the stage for both challenges and adaptations in the centuries that followed. This period of decline would ultimately shape the character and trajectory of the city, influencing its responses to future global developments.

The French Occupation

The French occupation of Amsterdam from 1795 to 1813 marked a significant chapter in the city's history, intertwining its fate with the broader currents of European politics and reshaping its social, economic, and administrative landscape. This period began when the Batavian Republic was established, effectively aligning the Netherlands with revolutionary France. The transition was not merely a change in governance; it was a transformation that would leave an indelible mark on Amsterdam's identity.

Under Napoleonic rule, the city experienced a series of sweeping reforms that aimed to modernize its political structure and align it more closely with French ideals. The most notable change was the introduction of a centralized administrative system that replaced the fragmented governance of the previous Dutch Republic. The new regime sought to impose a uniform legal and administrative framework across the Netherlands, leading to the establishment of new municipal structures and the introduction of the Napoleonic Code. This legal framework not only streamlined the legal process but also emphasized principles such as equality before the law and the protection of property rights, ideals that resonated with the revolutionary spirit of the time.

Economically, the French occupation had a dual effect on Amsterdam. Initially, the city benefited from the abolition of trade barriers and the establishment of direct trade links with France and its colonies, which opened new markets for Dutch goods. This period saw a temporary surge in commerce, particularly in textiles and colonial products. However, this economic boon was short-lived as the broader European conflict, particularly the Continental System—Napoleon's blockade designed to cripple the British economy—restricted trade and led to economic hardship. Amsterdam's merchants, who had thrived on international trade, found themselves increasingly constrained by the very policies that were initially designed to benefit them.

The social fabric of Amsterdam also underwent significant changes during the French occupation. The introduction of French educational reforms brought about a shift in the education system, promoting secularism and the inclusion of modern subjects, which had lasting effects on Dutch education. However, the period was also marked by social unrest; popular discontent grew against the French authorities, fueled by the conscription of Dutch citizens into the French military and the imposition of heavy taxes to support the war efforts. This unrest culminated in a series of protests and riots, reflecting the growing dissatisfaction with foreign rule.

Culturally, the French occupation had a profound impact on Amsterdam. The city saw an influx of French culture, which influenced art, literature, and fashion. The establishment of the National Museum of Antiquities in 1800 and the introduction of various artistic movements can be traced back to this period. However, traditional Dutch culture faced challenges as the French sought to impose their own cultural norms, leading to a complex interplay between resistance and adaptation among the local populace.

The end of the French occupation came in 1813, following Napoleon's defeat and the subsequent withdrawal of French troops. The aftermath of the occupation left Amsterdam with a mixed legacy. While the administrative and legal reforms contributed to the modernization of the city, the economic disruptions and social tensions fostered by the occupation left scars that would take years to heal. In the wake of the occupation, Amsterdam emerged not only as a city that had weathered the storms of war but also as one that had been irrevocably changed, setting the stage for its future growth and development in the 19th century.

In conclusion, the French occupation of Amsterdam was a transformative period that reshaped the city's political, economic, and cultural landscape. It highlighted the tensions between local traditions and foreign impositions, a theme that would continue to resonate in Amsterdam's subsequent history. The legacy of this era is evident in the city's ongoing evolution, influencing its trajectory into a modern, resilient urban center.

Economic and Social Changes in Amsterdam during the 18th Century

The 18th century marked a period of significant transformation for Amsterdam as it navigated the complexities of a shifting economic landscape and evolving social dynamics. This era, often regarded as one of decline in terms of Dutch global dominance, nevertheless exhibited resilience and adaptability within the city, particularly in trade, industry, and societal structure.

Shifts in Trade

The decline of the Dutch Republic's global power, particularly in the wake of the Anglo-Dutch Wars, had profound implications for Amsterdam's trade. The once-thriving mercantile empire that characterized the previous century began to fragment, leading to increased competition from emerging maritime powers such as Britain and France. As a result, Amsterdam's status as a dominant trading port diminished. The city increasingly relied on its historical trade routes, particularly those involving the Baltic and the North Sea, but faced challenges in maintaining the volume and profitability of its trade.

The rise of the English and the French colonial empires further eroded Amsterdam's economic stronghold. However, the city adapted by diversifying its trade portfolio, focusing more on intra-European commerce and the importation of raw materials, which could be processed locally. The establishment of new trade connections with regions like the Caribbean and the Americas became vital, as merchants sought to capitalize on the lucrative sugar and tobacco markets.

Industrial Development

Although Amsterdam did not experience industrialization to the same extent as other European cities in the 18th century, early forms of industry began to take shape. The textile industry, particularly wool and linen production, became increasingly significant, as local workshops proliferated. The introduction of mechanized processes, albeit limited, marked the beginnings of industrial change.

The latter part of the century saw the emergence of new industries, including shipbuilding and the production of machinery, which laid the groundwork for future industrialization in the 19th century. This shift was essential as it provided employment opportunities for a growing urban population, even as traditional industries faced decline.

Social Changes

The economic transformations of the 18th century precipitated significant social changes. Amsterdam's population grew, fueled by both rural migration and immigration from other parts of Europe. This demographic shift contributed to a burgeoning working class, leading to a more diverse and stratified society. The influx of people brought new cultural influences but also intensified competition for jobs and housing, resulting in rising tensions among various social groups.

Social stratification became increasingly pronounced, with a clear divide between the wealthy merchant class and the laboring poor. The opulence of the merchant elite was juxtaposed against the harsh realities faced by the working class, who often lived in overcrowded conditions. This disparity fostered discontent, leading to the beginnings of labor movements and calls for social reform later in the century.

The 18th century also witnessed the rise of Enlightenment thought, which began to permeate Amsterdam's social fabric. This intellectual movement emphasized reason, science, and individual rights, challenging traditional hierarchies and advocating for social progress. The ideas of philosophers such as Spinoza and Locke found resonance among Amsterdam's burgeoning middle class, inspiring movements for civic rights and increased political engagement.

Conclusion

In summary, the 18th century was a period of adaptation and transformation for Amsterdam. While the city grappled with the decline of its global trading power, it began to diversify its economic activities and lay the groundwork for future industrialization. Socially, the period was defined by a growing awareness of class divisions and a burgeoning consciousness of rights and reforms. Together, these economic and social changes set the stage for Amsterdam's evolution into a modern city in the ensuing centuries, reflecting a complex interplay of decline and resilience.

The Impact of Enlightenment Ideas on Amsterdam's Intellectual and Political Landscape

The Enlightenment, a profound intellectual movement spanning the late 17th to the 18th century, significantly shaped Amsterdam's cultural and political fabric. As the ideas of reason, individualism, and skepticism of tradition permeated European thought, Amsterdam emerged as a critical hub for Enlightenment philosophies. This period marked a transition from dogmatic belief systems to an era that celebrated rational inquiry and human rights, influencing various facets of Amsterdam's society.

One of the most notable impacts of Enlightenment ideas in Amsterdam was the flourishing of intellectual discourse. The city was home to a vibrant community of philosophers, scientists, and writers, many of whom contributed to the broader European Enlightenment. Figures such as Baruch Spinoza, a major philosopher of the time, laid the groundwork for modern secular thought, advocating for the separation of philosophy from religious dogma. His writings encouraged critical thinking and the questioning of established beliefs, resonating with the Enlightenment's emphasis on reason.

Moreover, the presence of the Amsterdam Public Library and various salons facilitated the exchange of Enlightenment ideas. These venues became centers for discussion and debate, where citizens engaged with new concepts about democracy, civil rights, and social contracts. The writings of John Locke, Jean-Jacques Rousseau, and Voltaire circulated widely, inspiring local thinkers and activists to advocate for reforms in governance and society. The dissemination of these ideas fostered a culture of intellectual inquiry that permeated the arts, sciences, and politics.

In the political realm, the Enlightenment encouraged a shift towards more democratic forms of governance, challenging the traditional autocratic rule prevalent in Europe. Amsterdam's merchant class, empowered by trade and economic prosperity, began to advocate for greater political representation and civic rights. The principles of popular sovereignty and the social contract found traction among Amsterdam's citizens, promoting the idea that governments should be accountable to the people. This ideological shift laid the groundwork for the city's active involvement in the broader political transformations that characterized the Dutch Republic.

The Enlightenment also spurred advancements in education and science in Amsterdam. The establishment of institutions like the Athenaeum Illustre in 1632, which later became the University of Amsterdam, reflected the growing importance placed on education as a means to cultivate rational thought and informed citizenship. Scientific inquiry flourished during this period, with notable figures such as Antonie van Leeuwenhoek, who is often referred to as the father of microbiology, making significant contributions to the understanding of the natural world. His work embodied the Enlightenment spirit of inquiry, emphasizing observation and empirical evidence.

Additionally, the Enlightenment's focus on individual rights and liberties influenced social movements within Amsterdam. As ideas about personal freedom and equality gained prominence, calls for the abolition of practices such as slavery and the promotion of civil rights emerged. Enlightenment thinkers argued for the inherent dignity of all individuals, leading to increased advocacy for marginalized groups within the city.

Despite the positive influences of Enlightenment thought, it is essential to acknowledge the tensions it created. The challenges posed to established authorities often led to backlash from conservative factions within society, igniting debates over the role of tradition and the church in public life. However, these conflicts ultimately contributed to a more dynamic civic discourse, encouraging active participation in political and social reform.

In conclusion, the Enlightenment profoundly influenced Amsterdam's intellectual and political landscape, fostering a culture of reasoned debate, scientific inquiry, and social reform. The city became a beacon of Enlightenment thought, shaping its identity and values as a forward-thinking society. As Amsterdam navigated the complexities of modernization and governance, the legacy of Enlightenment ideals continued to resonate, informing its trajectory into the modern era.

Urban Development and Population Growth in 18th Century Amsterdam

The 18th century marked a transformative period for Amsterdam, characterized by significant urban development and demographic changes that shaped the city's layout and social fabric. While the previous century had seen Amsterdam's Golden Age, the 18th century was a time of decline for Dutch power, yet it also laid the groundwork for future growth and modernization.

Urban Expansion

As Amsterdam transitioned into the 18th century, the city experienced a gradual shift from its medieval core. The original layout, shaped by the famous concentric canals, began to expand outward in response to a growing population and the need for more living and working spaces. The city's architecture reflected this expansion, with new neighborhoods emerging that featured a mix of residential and commercial buildings. The once predominantly merchant-oriented city started to see a diversification of its urban landscape, accommodating artisans, laborers, and the burgeoning middle class.

By mid-century, Amsterdam's urban development was marked by the construction of new residential areas such as the Jordaan and the expansion of existing neighborhoods. The Jordaan, originally developed for the working class, became a melting pot of lower-middle-class families, artists, and immigrants. This neighborhood not only exemplified the physical expansion of Amsterdam but also illustrated the social changes occurring within the city as diverse communities began to coalesce.

Demographic Changes

The population of Amsterdam during the 18th century was characterized by a complex interplay of migration, urbanization, and socio-economic shifts. By the early 1700s, the population was estimated to be around 200,000, making Amsterdam one of the most populous cities in Europe at the time. However, the population dynamics were influenced by various factors, including economic downturns and fluctuating trade patterns.

The decline of the Dutch East India Company (VOC) in the late 17th century resulted in reduced economic prosperity and job opportunities, leading to stagnation in population growth. Nevertheless, Amsterdam remained an attractive destination for migrants, particularly those from rural areas of the Netherlands and neighboring regions. The promise of work and the allure of urban life continued to draw individuals to the city, resulting in a complex demographic tapestry.

This influx of new residents challenged the city's infrastructure and housing availability. Rapid urbanization led to overcrowding, particularly in the working-class neighborhoods. Tenement housing, often of poor quality, emerged to accommodate the growing population, exacerbating social inequalities and contributing to public health challenges. The local government was increasingly pressured to address these issues, initiating public health reforms and infrastructure improvements.

Social and Economic Implications

The urban development and population growth in 18th-century Amsterdam had significant social implications. As the merchant elite consolidated wealth, social stratification became more pronounced. The disparities between the affluent and the impoverished were starkly visible, with opulent canal houses standing in contrast to the cramped living conditions of the working class.

Moreover, the demographic changes fostered a sense of community among the working-class residents, as they banded together for mutual support in the face of economic challenges. The emergence of guilds and trade unions began to take shape during this period, laying the foundation for future labor movements.

In summary, the 18th century was a pivotal period for Amsterdam, marked by urban development and demographic changes that influenced the city's layout and social structure. While the shadows of economic decline loomed large, the resilience of its population and the dynamic urban environment set the stage for the transformations that would follow in the 19th century. The growth and adaptation during this time highlighted the enduring complexity of Amsterdam's identity as a city that continually evolved in response to internal and external challenges.

Chapter 4

The 19th Century and Industrialization

The Kingdom of the Netherlands

The defeat of Napoleon in 1815 marked a pivotal moment in European history, leading to significant political transformations across the continent. In the aftermath of the Napoleonic Wars, the Congress of Vienna sought to restore stability by redrawing national boundaries and establishing a balance of power. As a result, the Kingdom of the Netherlands was formed, uniting the northern and southern provinces of the Netherlands under a constitutional monarchy. This newly established state would have profound implications for Amsterdam, which, as the largest city and a key economic center, played a crucial role in shaping the kingdom's identity, governance, and socio-economic landscape.

Amsterdam had long been a hub of commerce and trade, flourishing during the Dutch Golden Age. However, the Napoleonic Wars had significantly disrupted its economic activities. The British naval blockade and the continental system imposed by Napoleon hampered trade routes, leading to economic decline and social unrest. Following the wars, the restoration of peace allowed Amsterdam to reassert its position as a commercial powerhouse within the new kingdom. The city leveraged its established mercantile networks, enabling it to quickly rebound from the wartime economic slump. The reopening of trade routes led to a surge in maritime commerce, bolstering Amsterdam's economy and enhancing its importance within the Kingdom of the Netherlands.

As the capital of the new kingdom, Amsterdam became the political and cultural heart of the nation. The establishment of the Dutch monarchy under King William I in 1815 further solidified Amsterdam's status. The king recognized the city's significance in fostering national unity and promoting economic growth. Consequently, Amsterdam was the site of various national institutions, including the royal palace, governmental offices, and the central bank, which facilitated the administration of the new state. This concentration of power and resources in Amsterdam fostered a sense of identity and pride among its inhabitants and positioned the city as a leader in national affairs.

The 19th century also witnessed considerable urban development in Amsterdam, driven by the need to accommodate a growing population and support its emerging industrial economy. The city underwent significant infrastructural transformations, including the expansion of the canal system, which facilitated trade and transportation. Additionally, the construction of new residential areas and public buildings reflected the aspirations of a burgeoning middle class and the city's ambition to modernize. This urban expansion was crucial for integrating Amsterdam into the broader socio-economic fabric of the kingdom, as it attracted workers and entrepreneurs seeking opportunities in the revitalized economy.

Moreover, Amsterdam played a vital role in the cultural renaissance of the Netherlands during this period. The city became a center for the arts, education, and intellectual discourse, fostering a vibrant cultural scene that reflected the values of the new state. Institutions such as the University of Amsterdam and various art galleries and museums emerged, contributing to the nation's cultural capital. The flourishing of Dutch literature, visual arts, and philosophy during this time further enhanced Amsterdam's reputation as a beacon of enlightenment and progress.

In summary, Amsterdam's role in the newly formed Kingdom of the Netherlands after the defeat of Napoleon was multifaceted. The city not only regained its economic prominence but also became the political and cultural epicenter of the nation. The transformative developments in urban infrastructure, governance, and cultural life laid the groundwork for Amsterdam to evolve into a modern metropolis, shaping its trajectory in the subsequent decades. The legacy of this period continues to influence Amsterdam's identity and its pivotal role within the Netherlands today.

Industrialization and Economic Change

The 19th century was a pivotal period in the history of Amsterdam, marked by the profound transformations brought about by industrialization. The advent of industrialization in the Netherlands—especially in cities like Amsterdam—was fueled by a combination of factors including technological advancements, the changing nature of labor, and evolving economic structures. This era not only reshaped the economic landscape of Amsterdam but also significantly influenced its social fabric and the lives of its inhabitants.

At the outset of the 19th century, Amsterdam was primarily a center of trade and commerce. The city had built its wealth on maritime trade, particularly through the activities of the Dutch East India Company in the previous century. However, the landscape began to shift as industrialization took root. The introduction of steam power and mechanization dramatically altered production processes, leading to the rise of factories and mass production. Amsterdam, with its established infrastructure and access to maritime routes, quickly adapted to these changes.

The textile industry emerged as one of the most significant sectors during this period, alongside shipbuilding and machinery manufacturing. Factories began to sprout across the city, drawing in workers from rural areas as the demand for labor surged. This influx of workers transformed Amsterdam's demographics; the city's population grew rapidly as it became a magnet for those seeking economic opportunities. By the mid-19th century, Amsterdam's population had doubled compared to earlier decades, resulting in intensified urbanization.

This industrial boom had profound implications for the workforce. Traditional artisan crafts began to decline as factory-based production took precedence, leading to a shift in labor dynamics. Many skilled artisans found themselves at a disadvantage, unable to compete with the efficiency of mechanized production. Consequently, the workforce became increasingly stratified, leading to the emergence of a working class that often faced harsh conditions. Factories operated long hours, and workers endured minimal wages, which sparked the beginning of labor movements advocating for rights and better working conditions.

The economic changes spurred by industrialization also led to significant social reform movements. Workers began to organize themselves into unions and associations, demanding fair wages, reasonable working hours, and improved conditions. The rise of socialism in the late 19th century found strong support in Amsterdam, where labor activism flourished. This social unrest was a response to the disparities created by industrial capitalism, as inequality became more pronounced in the rapidly growing city.

In addition to social movements, industrialization also fostered a cultural renaissance in Amsterdam. The newfound wealth generated by industrial enterprises contributed to investments in education, arts, and public infrastructure. The city saw the establishment of cultural institutions and the proliferation of artistic movements, which reflected the diverse experiences and aspirations of its burgeoning population. The late 19th century witnessed the rise of notable artists and intellectuals who navigated the complexities of a society in transition, capturing the essence of Amsterdam's evolving identity.

Despite the challenges that accompanied industrialization, it also positioned Amsterdam as a key player in the global economy. The city's strategic location allowed it to serve as a hub for international trade, facilitating the exchange of goods and ideas. The development of transportation networks, including railways and improved shipping routes, further integrated Amsterdam into a broader economic framework, solidifying its status as a vital economic center in Europe.

In conclusion, the rise of industry in Amsterdam during the 19th century marked a transformative phase in the city's history. It spurred economic growth, reshaped the workforce, and catalyzed social reform movements, while also laying the groundwork for Amsterdam's emergence as a modern urban center. The legacies of this period—both positive and negative—continue to influence the city's development and identity to this day.

Social Reform Movements in 19th Century Amsterdam

The 19th century was a transformative era for Amsterdam, characterized by rapid industrialization, urbanization, and significant social change. As the city evolved from a primarily mercantile economy to one increasingly dominated by industry and the service sector, the social fabric of Amsterdam began to shift dramatically. The emergence of social reform movements during this time reflected the growing awareness of inequalities and injustices faced by the working class, ultimately laying the groundwork for labor unions, socialism, and other reform initiatives.

Labor Unions and the Right to Organize

The rise of the industrial economy created new job opportunities, but it also led to harsh working conditions, long hours, and meager wages for many laborers. Factories, shipyards, and other industrial workplaces often lacked basic safety measures, and workers had little recourse for addressing grievances. Amidst these challenges, the labor movement began to gain traction.

By the mid-19th century, workers in Amsterdam started organizing themselves into trade unions, which aimed to improve labor conditions and secure better wages. The first significant labor union in the Netherlands, the Dutch Labor Union (Algemeene Nederlandsche Arbeidersvereniging, ANAV), was founded in 1871. This organization marked a pivotal moment in Amsterdam's labor history, as it provided a platform for workers to collectively voice their demands and advocate for their rights. The establishment of labor unions not only empowered workers but also fostered solidarity among different trade groups, contributing to a sense of collective identity and purpose.

The Rise of Socialism

Parallel to the labor movement, socialist ideologies began to take root in Amsterdam, influenced by broader European trends. Socialism emerged as a response to the perceived failures of capitalism, particularly regarding the exploitation of the working class and the widening gap between the rich and poor. Amsterdam became a hub for socialist thought, with intellectuals, activists, and labor leaders advocating for radical changes to the socio-economic system.

The establishment of the Dutch Social Democratic Workers' Party (SDAP) in 1894 marked a significant milestone in the socialist movement. The SDAP sought to represent the interests of the working class within the political system and aimed to achieve reform through parliamentary means, contrasting with more revolutionary approaches favored by some factions. The party's advocacy for progressive policies, such as universal suffrage, social welfare, and labor rights, resonated with many in Amsterdam, leading to increased political engagement among the working class.

Other Reform Movements

In addition to labor unions and socialism, Amsterdam saw the emergence of other social reform movements addressing various issues, including women's rights, education, and public health. The late 19th century was a period of heightened awareness regarding women's roles in society. Activists campaigned for women's suffrage, better access to education, and improvements in working conditions for women, particularly in factories and domestic work.

Furthermore, reformers began to advocate for public health initiatives, recognizing the dire conditions in which many working-class families lived. The rise of urban poverty prompted calls for better housing, sanitation, and public health measures. Groups focused on improving the living conditions in the city, pushing for reforms that would address the needs of the urban poor.

Legacy of Social Reform Movements

The social reform movements of 19th-century Amsterdam played a crucial role in shaping the city's political landscape and social policies in the years to come. They not only empowered the working class but also laid the foundation for future social welfare systems and labor rights legislation. The legacy of these movements is evident in modern Amsterdam, where the city continues to champion social equity, worker rights, and progressive policies that reflect its historical commitment to social reform.

In summary, the emergence of labor unions, socialism, and other reform movements in 19th-century Amsterdam was a response to the challenges posed by industrialization and urbanization. These movements not only addressed immediate concerns related to labor conditions and social justice but also contributed to the broader discourse on equality and human rights that continues to resonate in contemporary society.

Urbanization and Housing

The 19th century marked a significant turning point for Amsterdam, characterized by rapid urbanization driven by industrialization and an influx of migrants seeking employment and better living conditions. This period saw the population of Amsterdam swell dramatically, leading to unprecedented challenges in urban planning and housing provision.

As factories sprung up and the economy shifted from agriculture to industry, the city attracted workers from rural areas and other parts of Europe. By the late 19th century, Amsterdam's population had doubled, and the city faced an urgent need to accommodate this surge. The existing housing stock was inadequate, often comprising cramped and unsanitary conditions. Many workers were forced to live in overcrowded tenements, which contributed to public health crises, including outbreaks of diseases such as cholera and typhoid.

The inadequacy of housing prompted civic leaders and urban planners to take action. One of the responses to the housing crisis was the development of new housing projects aimed at improving living conditions for the working class. These initiatives included the construction of 'tuinwijken' or garden neighborhoods, which were designed to provide healthier living environments with access to green spaces. The garden city movement, inspired by concepts from Britain, influenced these developments, emphasizing the importance of light, air, and community.

In the early 20th century, the municipality began to implement comprehensive urban planning strategies, which included zoning laws and building regulations. This marked a departure from the ad hoc developments of the previous decades. The city sought to create a more organized urban landscape that could accommodate the growing population while maintaining public health and aesthetic standards. Architects and planners began to design residential neighborhoods that balanced density with livability, emphasizing spacious layouts and communal areas.

However, the rapid urbanization also led to challenges beyond just housing. The infrastructure of Amsterdam struggled to keep pace with the growing population. Public transport systems, sanitation, and waste management faced significant strains, leading to traffic congestion and environmental issues. The city's narrow streets and historic layout were ill-equipped for modern demands, necessitating innovative solutions to integrate the new with the old.

As the 20th century progressed, the post-World War II era brought another wave of urbanization, compounded by the arrival of new immigrants and a housing shortage exacerbated by wartime destruction. The government intervened once again, launching extensive public housing projects to provide affordable accommodation. These developments, often characterized by functionalist architecture, aimed to address the needs of diverse populations, including low-income families and single residents.

Despite these efforts, the housing market in Amsterdam continued to face challenges. The late 20th century saw a shift in focus towards privatization and deregulation, which led to rising property prices and a gradual transformation of the city's character. Gentrification became a pressing issue, as affluent residents moved into historically working-class neighborhoods, driving up rents and displacing long-term residents.

In response to these challenges, contemporary urban policies have increasingly focused on sustainability and inclusivity. The city has embraced innovative housing solutions, such as cooperative housing models and mixed-use developments that integrate residential and commercial spaces. Moreover, Amsterdam's commitment to sustainability has led to initiatives promoting energy-efficient buildings and green roofs, reflecting a growing awareness of environmental impacts.

In conclusion, the urbanization of Amsterdam has been marked by a complex interplay of social, economic, and political factors. The challenges of rapid growth have necessitated continual adaptation and innovation in housing policies, reflecting the city's resilience and commitment to creating a livable environment for all its residents. As Amsterdam continues to evolve, the lessons learned from its history of urbanization and housing development will undoubtedly shape its future urban landscape.

Cultural and Artistic Renaissance

The late 19th century marked a significant period of cultural and artistic revival in Amsterdam, characterized by an effervescent reawakening in the arts, literature, and education. This renaissance emerged from a confluence of factors, including industrialization, increased urbanization, and the influence of broader European movements. As Amsterdam transitioned into a modern metropolis, it became a nurturing ground for creativity and intellectual advancement.

One of the most notable aspects of this revival was the flourishing of the visual arts. The establishment of the Amsterdam School in architecture signified a departure from traditional styles toward a more expressive, functional design that embraced brickwork and dynamic forms. This architectural movement was not only a reflection of the changing urban landscape but also an embodiment of the city's cultural aspirations. Key figures such as Hendrik Petrus Berlage played a pivotal role in this movement, advocating for designs that integrated art with everyday life. Berlage's Stock Exchange building (Beurs van Berlage), completed in 1903, stands as a testament to this period, showcasing a blend of functionality and aesthetic appeal.

36

Moreover, the late 19th century saw the rise of Impressionism and Post-Impressionism in the Dutch art scene. The works of painters like Vincent van Gogh and Maurits Cornelis Escher, though they would not gain widespread recognition until later, began to influence local artists and offer new perspectives on color, light, and form. Van Gogh's connection to Amsterdam—his early life and education—provided a contextual backdrop for the city's artistic evolution, as young artists sought inspiration from his innovative techniques and emotive subject matter.

Literature also flourished during this era, with the emergence of significant literary figures such as Louis Couperus and Herman Gorter. Their works often explored themes of individualism, society, and the human condition, reflecting the broader European literary trends of realism and symbolism. This literary renaissance was supported by the founding of institutions such as the Amsterdam Library and the establishment of various literary salons, which fostered dialogue and exchange among writers, poets, and thinkers.

In addition to the visual arts and literature, the late 19th century was a period of educational reform in Amsterdam. The University of Amsterdam, which had been established in 1632, began to expand its focus on research and modern academic disciplines. This shift not only elevated the level of education available in the city but also contributed to a more informed and culturally engaged populace. The establishment of technical schools and art academies also ensured that a new generation of artists and intellectuals received the training necessary to contribute to the vibrant cultural milieu.

Cultural institutions played a vital role in this renaissance. The Rijksmuseum, which underwent significant renovations during this period, became a beacon of Dutch heritage and art, housing an impressive collection that included masterpieces from the Dutch Golden Age. The museum's focus on both historical and contemporary art encouraged public engagement and appreciation for the arts, setting the stage for Amsterdam's future as a cultural capital.

The late 19th century in Amsterdam was thus a transformative period characterized by a rich tapestry of artistic expression and intellectual growth. The city's commitment to nurturing the arts and education during this time laid the groundwork for its future cultural prominence, fostering an environment that celebrated creativity, innovation, and the exchange of ideas. This cultural and artistic renaissance not only enriched Amsterdam's identity but also influenced the broader cultural landscape of the Netherlands and beyond, leaving an enduring legacy that continues to resonate today.

Chapter 5

Amsterdam and World War I

The Netherlands' Neutrality

During World War I (1914-1918), the geopolitical landscape of Europe was fraught with tension and conflict, yet the Netherlands managed to maintain its neutrality throughout the war. This position not only shaped the experiences of Amsterdam, the nation's capital, but it also had far-reaching implications for the city's social, economic, and cultural fabric during this tumultuous period.

The roots of Dutch neutrality can be traced back to historical precedents established during previous conflicts, notably the Napoleonic Wars. The Dutch government, recognizing the devastation wrought by military engagement, adopted a policy of neutrality that aimed to protect its sovereignty and maintain peace within its borders. This stance was reinforced by the Dutch constitution, which enshrined neutrality as a guiding principle of foreign policy. As a result, when World War I erupted, the Netherlands declared its neutrality, a decision that was met with mixed reactions domestically and internationally.

Amsterdam, as the largest city in the Netherlands, became a focal point for the complexities of this neutrality. The city was not only a hub of commerce and trade but also a center for political discourse. Many citizens supported neutrality, believing it was in the best interest of the nation to avoid the carnage that engulfed neighboring countries. However, there were also voices within the society that advocated for support towards the Allies, particularly due to ideological affinities and historical ties.

The economic implications of neutrality were significant for Amsterdam. As European nations descended into conflict, the city experienced a surge in trade activities. Amsterdam's strategic location made it an ideal point for shipping goods, and the port became a bustling center for importing and exporting a wide array of products, including food, textiles, and raw materials. The Netherlands became a crucial supplier to countries at war, particularly Germany and the Allies. This influx of trade brought prosperity to Amsterdam, as businesses capitalized on the demand for goods that could not be sourced from war-torn regions. However, this economic boom was not without its challenges, as the city faced pressures related to scarce resources, inflation, and the difficulties of maintaining supply lines.

Socially, Amsterdam's neutrality fostered a sense of national identity, as citizens rallied around the idea of a peaceful and independent Netherlands. The war prompted a wave of humanitarian efforts, with organizations and citizens mobilizing to support Belgium, which was devastated by German occupation. This led to increased solidarity among the Dutch population and a commitment to aid those affected by the war, showcasing Amsterdam's role as a compassionate neighbor despite its official stance of neutrality.

Culturally, the war years also had a profound impact on Amsterdam. The city became a refuge for artists, intellectuals, and dissidents fleeing from neighboring countries. This influx enriched Amsterdam's cultural landscape, leading to a fusion of ideas and artistic expressions. The war prompted reflections on themes of peace, conflict, and human resilience, which permeated the artistic works of the time.

However, the end of the war did not conclude the challenges faced by Amsterdam. The post-war period brought about economic difficulties and social tensions, as returning soldiers and the resumption of normal trade led to competition for jobs and resources. Nevertheless, the experiences of World War I solidified Amsterdam's identity as a neutral city, influencing its future interactions on the global stage.

In summary, Amsterdam's navigation of neutrality during World War I was a complex interplay of economic, social, and cultural factors. The city's ability to maintain its stance amidst the chaos of war contributed to its development as a significant European center, with lasting implications that would resonate in the years to come. This unique position not only shaped Amsterdam's identity during the war but also laid the groundwork for its future as a hub of peace and diplomacy in a rapidly changing world.

Economic Impact of the War

World War I, which lasted from 1914 to 1918, had a profound impact on nations around the globe, including the Netherlands, which maintained a position of neutrality throughout the conflict. However, even as a neutral country, Amsterdam felt the ripples of war in various aspects of its economy, trade, and the daily lives of its citizens.

Trade Disruptions

Amsterdam had long been a vital hub for international trade, owing to its strategic location and extensive maritime network. However, the war resulted in significant disruptions to global shipping routes. The British naval blockade aimed at Germany severely restricted the flow of goods into and out of Europe. As a result, Amsterdam's merchants faced increased difficulties in sourcing raw materials and exporting finished goods. The city's economy, heavily reliant on trade, suffered as key industries, such as textiles and shipbuilding, experienced a downturn. The scarcity of imported goods led to inflated prices, creating a strain on both businesses and consumers.

The war also prompted the Dutch government to implement regulations aimed at managing resources. Rationing measures were introduced for food and essential commodities, which further complicated trade dynamics. As a result, many businesses struggled to adapt to the new economic reality, leading to layoffs and increased unemployment in the city.

Industrial Changes

With the disruption of international trade, Amsterdam's industries faced considerable challenges. Factories that depended on imported raw materials often had to cut back on production or even shut down completely. However, some sectors saw a temporary boost due to the war; for instance, the manufacturing of munitions and military supplies became more prominent, albeit in a limited capacity. This shift provided jobs for some citizens but was not nearly enough to offset the broader economic decline.

Furthermore, the war catalyzed changes in labor dynamics. As men were conscripted into military service, the workforce inevitably shifted. Women began to fill roles that had traditionally been occupied by men, marking a significant social change. This shift not only contributed to the war effort but also laid the groundwork for future social reform movements advocating for gender equality in the workplace.

Daily Life and Social Impact

The economic strain of World War I extended into the daily lives of Amsterdam's residents. With rationing in place, citizens faced shortages of basic necessities such as bread, meat, and dairy products. The city saw the emergence of black markets, where goods were sold at exorbitant prices, further exacerbating social inequalities.

Public sentiment during this period was mixed. While many supported the government's neutral stance, there was also a palpable sense of discontent among the working class. Strikes became more common as workers protested against wage cuts and poor working conditions exacerbated by the economic downturn. The growing discontent eventually contributed to a rise in political activism and the emergence of socialist movements in the city.

Moreover, the war prompted a cultural response that reflected the struggles of the time. Artists, writers, and intellectuals began to question societal values, leading to a flourishing of critical discourse and a reevaluation of national identity in a post-war context. This intellectual ferment would prove significant in shaping Amsterdam's cultural landscape in the years that followed.

Conclusion

The economic impact of World War I on Amsterdam was multifaceted, leading to trade disruptions, industrial changes, and significant alterations in daily life for its citizens. While the city managed to maintain its neutrality, the war's consequences echoed through its economy and social fabric, influencing the trajectory of Amsterdam in the interwar period and beyond. The lessons learned during this tumultuous time would set the stage for the challenges and transformations that lay ahead in the evolving narrative of this vibrant city.

Social Tensions and Strikes

The period surrounding World War I was marked by significant social tensions and widespread unrest in Amsterdam, reflecting broader socio-economic conditions and political currents in the Netherlands and Europe. As the war ravaged Europe from 1914 to 1918, the Netherlands maintained a stance of neutrality, which had profound implications for its economy and social fabric. However, the neutrality did not shield Amsterdam from the war's socio-economic fallout, leading to heightened social tensions and an environment ripe for political activism.

One of the primary catalysts for social unrest in Amsterdam during this period was the economic strain brought on by the war. Though the country was technically neutral, the war disrupted trade routes and caused shortages of essential goods, such as food and materials. The blockade imposed by the Allies hampered imports, leading to skyrocketing prices and inflation. As the cost of living increased, wages stagnated for many workers, exacerbating feelings of discontent and resentment. The working class, already grappling with poor working conditions and long hours, found themselves in a precarious situation, facing the dual threats of economic hardship and the looming specter of war.

In response to these mounting pressures, labor movements in Amsterdam began to mobilize more aggressively. Strikes became a common tool of protest as workers sought to improve their working conditions, wages, and access to basic necessities. The Amsterdam dockworkers, for example, organized strikes to demand better pay and working conditions, highlighting the critical role of labor in the city's economy. These strikes often garnered public support, as other sectors of society recognized the shared struggles of the working class.

The emergence of political activism during this time was also significant. The rise of socialist and labor parties in the Netherlands created a platform for voicing the grievances of the working class. Organizations such as the Dutch Socialist Party (SDAP) gained traction, advocating for workers' rights and broader social reforms. Political rallies and demonstrations became more frequent, as activists sought to mobilize public opinion against the government's inaction regarding social issues exacerbated by the war.

One notable event was the 1918 general strike, which was sparked by the frustrations of workers over the worsening economic conditions and the government's failure to address their needs. This strike, which extended beyond Amsterdam to cities across the Netherlands, was marked by mass participation and solidarity among various labor unions and political groups. The general strike underscored a growing awareness among workers of their collective power and the potential to effect change through unity.

In the aftermath of the war, the social tensions that had simmered during the conflict did not dissipate. The post-war period saw a continuation of labor unrest as workers sought to secure the gains they had fought for, while the economic landscape remained fraught with challenges. The 1920s brought about a series of strikes that reflected ongoing grievances, with demands for better wages and working conditions continuing to resonate throughout the labor movement.

Furthermore, the period also saw the rise of other social movements, including those advocating for women's suffrage and rights, anti-colonial activism, and other progressive causes. The interwar years were characterized by a complex interplay of social movements seeking to address the inequalities and injustices exposed by the war and its aftermath.

In summary, the social tensions and strikes in Amsterdam during and after World War I were emblematic of a larger struggle for rights and recognition among the working class. Economic hardship, political activism, and a desire for social reform converged to create an environment of unrest that would shape Amsterdam's social landscape for years to come. This period laid the groundwork for significant changes in labor rights and social policies in the Netherlands, reflecting the lessons learned from the collective struggles of its citizens.

The Post-War Recovery

Following the devastation of World War I, Amsterdam faced significant challenges that required both economic and social rejuvenation. The effects of the war were felt profoundly, even though the Netherlands maintained an official stance of neutrality. Amsterdam's economy, heavily reliant on trade and commerce, experienced disruptions in supply chains and markets, leading to economic instability and social unrest. The post-war recovery period, spanning the late 1910s into the mid-1920s, was marked by concerted efforts to revitalize the city across multiple dimensions.

42

Economic Reconstruction

The immediate aftermath of World War I saw a decline in traditional industries, such as shipbuilding and textiles, which had long been staples of Amsterdam's economy. The war had disrupted international trade routes, leading to shortages and inflation. In response, city planners and business leaders initiated strategic economic reforms aimed at revitalizing the local economy. Investments in infrastructure became a priority, with significant funds directed towards modernizing ports and transportation networks.

The introduction of the Marshall Plan in 1948, while post-World War II, set a precedent for international aid that would later influence Amsterdam's recovery efforts after WWI. During the post-war recovery of the early 1920s, local government and businesses sought to foster relationships with neighboring countries to re-establish trade routes and restore economic stability.

Social Dynamics and Labor Movements

Socially, the war had exacerbated existing tensions within Amsterdam's diverse population. The working class faced rising living costs and job insecurity, leading to increased labor activism. Strikes and protests became more frequent as workers demanded better wages and working conditions. Labor unions gained traction, advocating for the rights of workers in various sectors. This period saw the establishment of social democratic movements that would shape the city's political landscape for decades to come.

The post-war recovery also coincided with a shift in societal values. The end of the war brought about a greater focus on social welfare and the importance of community support systems. The city government began implementing social policies aimed at improving living conditions, healthcare, and education. Initiatives to address housing shortages were introduced, leading to the construction of new residential areas designed to accommodate the growing population.

Cultural Renaissance

Alongside economic and social recovery, the post-war period marked the beginning of a cultural renaissance in Amsterdam. The scars of war, coupled with the optimism of recovery, fostered a vibrant cultural scene. Artists, writers, and musicians began to flourish, contributing to a renewed sense of identity and community. The arts became a vital means of expression and reflection on the societal changes taking place.

The city's cultural institutions, including museums and theaters, played a pivotal role in this revival. The establishment of new galleries and performance spaces allowed local talent to showcase their work, while international artists found a welcoming environment to explore their creativity. This flourishing cultural scene not only enriched the life of the city but also attracted visitors, laying the groundwork for Amsterdam's emergence as a cultural capital in subsequent decades.

Conclusion

In summary, the post-war recovery of Amsterdam was a multifaceted process that involved economic revitalization, social reform, and a cultural renaissance. The city emerged from the shadows of World War I with a renewed sense of purpose, resilience, and creativity. The collective efforts of the government, labor movements, and cultural communities set the stage for Amsterdam's transformation into a modern city, capable of navigating the challenges of the interwar period and beyond. This era of recovery not only reinforced the importance of solidarity among the city's inhabitants but also highlighted the enduring capacity for regeneration in the face of adversity.

The Rise of Modern Amsterdam

The interwar period, spanning from 1918 to 1939, marked a significant transformation in Amsterdam, as the city began to modernize in response to a changing world. This era was characterized by an amalgamation of socio-economic shifts, technological advancements, and cultural evolution, all of which contributed to the rise of modern Amsterdam.

Economic Reconfiguration

Following the devastation of World War I, Amsterdam faced the challenge of economic recovery. The city, traditionally reliant on trade and finance, began to diversify its economic base. While the war had initially disrupted trade, the recovery period allowed the Netherlands to re-establish itself as a neutral trade hub. Amsterdam capitalized on this opportunity, leveraging its strategic geographic location to enhance trade routes and attract international businesses.

The city's port facilities underwent modernization, improving shipping and logistics capabilities. This development not only revitalized trade but also spurred related industries, such as shipbuilding and manufacturing, which became increasingly important to the local economy. As a result, Amsterdam transitioned from a primarily mercantile economy to a more industrialized one, laying the groundwork for future growth.

Urban Development and Infrastructure

As Amsterdam's population grew, driven by both natural increase and migration from rural areas, the city confronted significant housing shortages. To accommodate this influx, urban planners began to envision and implement large-scale housing projects, which reflected modern architectural styles. Notably, the Amsterdam School, an architectural movement that emerged during this time, emphasized functionalism, innovative design, and aesthetic integration with the urban environment.

Prominent examples of this movement include the social housing developments in the Spaarndammerbuurt, which combined affordability with artistic expression. These neighborhoods were designed with community in mind, incorporating green spaces and public amenities. This shift in urban planning not only addressed immediate housing needs but also fostered a sense of community and belonging among residents.

Cultural Flourishing

Culturally, the interwar years were a period of vibrant artistic and intellectual activity. Amsterdam became a crucible for avant-garde movements, with the arts flourishing across multiple disciplines. The city hosted influential figures in literature, theater, and visual arts, including writers like J. Slauerhoff and artists associated with the De Stijl movement, such as Piet Mondrian. The establishment of institutions like the Stedelijk Museum in 1938 showcased modern art and design, further solidifying Amsterdam's status as a cultural capital.

The period also witnessed the rise of experimental theater and cinema, with venues such as the Stadsschouwburg becoming hotbeds for new ideas and performances. This cultural dynamism reflected a broader societal shift towards modernity, where traditional norms were challenged, and new forms of expression emerged.

Social Change and Political Movements

The interwar period was not without its social tensions. Economic disparities became more pronounced, leading to the rise of labor movements and socialist organizations advocating for workers' rights and social justice. The establishment of trade unions and political parties aimed at addressing issues such as unemployment and housing conditions reflected a growing awareness of social inequalities.

Moreover, Amsterdam became a focal point for progressive politics, with various movements advocating for women's rights, education reform, and civil liberties. This activism not only shaped the political landscape of the city but also contributed to a broader dialogue about modern democracy and citizenship.

Conclusion

In summary, the interwar period marked a pivotal moment in the rise of modern Amsterdam. The city's economic diversification, urban development, cultural flourishing, and social movements collectively transformed its identity. As Amsterdam navigated the complexities of modernization, it laid the foundation for the dynamic, multicultural metropolis it is today. These developments not only redefined the cityscape but also set the stage for the challenges and opportunities that lay ahead in the tumultuous years that followed.

Chapter 6

Amsterdam during World War II

The German Occupation

The German occupation of Amsterdam during World War II, lasting from May 1940 until May 1945, profoundly impacted the city and its inhabitants, transforming Amsterdam into a landscape marked by fear, repression, and resistance. The Nazi regime implemented a series of policies that not only sought to control the population but also aimed to eradicate entire communities, particularly targeting the Jewish population.

Initially, the occupation seemed to bring about only minor inconveniences for the city's residents. However, as the Nazis solidified their control, life in Amsterdam began to deteriorate. The German authorities imposed strict regulations on everyday life, including curfews, censorship of the press, and the dissolution of political and social organizations that did not align with Nazi ideology. Public life was heavily surveilled, and citizens were encouraged to report any suspicious activities, fostering an atmosphere of mistrust and fear.

One of the most devastating impacts of the occupation was on Amsterdam's Jewish community. Before the war, Amsterdam was home to approximately 80,000 Jews, who contributed significantly to the city's cultural and economic life. However, following the implementation of anti-Semitic laws, Jews were systematically excluded from public life. They faced restrictions on their professions, were banned from public spaces, and were required to wear yellow stars to identify themselves. The situation escalated dramatically after the Nazis began mass deportations in 1942, sending thousands of Jews to concentration camps. By the end of the war, an estimated 75% of the Jewish population in Amsterdam had perished, a loss that left an indelible mark on the city's social fabric.

Resistance to the occupation emerged in various forms among the inhabitants of Amsterdam. Many citizens engaged in acts of defiance against the Nazi regime, including the distribution of underground newspapers, harboring Jewish families, and participating in sabotage activities. Notable resistance groups, such as the "Dutch Resistance," organized efforts to undermine German control, though these actions often came with severe reprisals. The Nazis responded with brutal crackdowns, executing suspected resistance members and conducting mass arrests, which further instilled a climate of terror.

A particularly poignant chapter of this period was the story of Anne Frank, a young Jewish girl who, along with her family, went into hiding in Amsterdam. The diary she kept during her time in hiding provides a personal perspective on the fears and aspirations of those living under occupation. Her eventual capture and deportation to Auschwitz highlighted the tragic fate that befell many Jews during this dark period.

The suffering experienced by the citizens of Amsterdam reached its zenith during the winter of 1944-1945, known as the "Hunger Winter." A combination of German blockades and the withdrawal of resources led to extreme food shortages, resulting in malnutrition and starvation. The city's inhabitants faced dire conditions, scavenging for food and relying on the black market to survive.

As the war drew to a close in 1945, Amsterdam experienced a sense of liberation, yet the aftermath of the occupation left deep scars. The city was physically damaged, with many buildings destroyed, and the psychological impact lingered long after the Nazis were expelled. The collective trauma of loss, especially among the Jewish community, and the moral implications of collaboration and resistance would shape Amsterdam's post-war identity.

In conclusion, the German occupation of Amsterdam was a period of profound suffering and moral complexity. The Nazi's systematic dehumanization of the Jewish population, the rise of resistance movements, and the extreme hardships endured by the general populace collectively transformed the city. The legacy of this tumultuous period continues to influence Amsterdam's cultural memory and its commitment to remembering the past as a means of ensuring that such atrocities are never repeated.

The Jewish Community and the Holocaust

Before World War II, Amsterdam was home to one of the largest and most vibrant Jewish communities in Europe. This community, which thrived for centuries, was characterized by a rich tapestry of cultural, religious, and intellectual contributions that significantly shaped the city's identity. The Jewish population of Amsterdam was a diverse group, comprising Ashkenazi Jews, Sephardic Jews, and immigrants from various parts of Europe, each adding their unique traditions and practices to the communal life. By the onset of World War II, approximately 80,000 Jews lived in the Netherlands, with a substantial number residing in Amsterdam.

The Nazi occupation of the Netherlands began in May 1940, and it brought with it a systematic campaign of anti-Semitic policies. The Amsterdam Jewish community faced increasing persecution, marked by the imposition of discriminatory laws, including the requirement for Jews to wear yellow stars, restrictions on their movement, and the confiscation of property.

These measures were part of a broader strategy to isolate and marginalize Jewish citizens, stripping them of their rights and dignity.

In July 1942, the situation escalated dramatically when the Nazis initiated mass deportations of Jews from Amsterdam to concentration camps. The first significant transport occurred on July 15, 1942, marking the beginning of a tragic period for the Jewish community. Families were torn apart, and individuals were forced to leave behind their homes and belongings, often with little warning. The deportations were characterized by a sense of terror, as the community was driven into hiding or into the clutches of the authorities. Estimates suggest that around 75% of the Jewish population in Amsterdam perished during the Holocaust, with many sent to Auschwitz, Sobibor, and other extermination camps.

The impact of the Holocaust on Amsterdam's Jewish community was profound and devastating. The vibrant cultural life that had flourished in the city was abruptly extinguished. Synagogues, schools, and community centers that had been the heart of Jewish life were closed and destroyed. The cultural contributions of Jewish artists, writers, and intellectuals were silenced, and a once-thriving community was reduced to a shadow of its former self. The loss was not only in numbers but also in the richness of cultural heritage that had been built over centuries.

Among the notable figures from Amsterdam's Jewish community was Anne Frank, whose diary has become a powerful testament to the horrors of the Holocaust and the resilience of the human spirit. Anne's experiences, documented in her diary while she and her family hid from the Nazis, provide a poignant insight into the daily struggles faced by Jews during this dark chapter of history. Her eventual capture and deportation serve as a stark reminder of the vulnerability of the Jewish population during the Holocaust.

After the war, Amsterdam's Jewish community faced the painful task of mourning their losses and rebuilding from the ruins. The absence of so many lives left a deep scar on the city, and the post-war period was marked by efforts to commemorate those who perished. Memorials, museums, and educational programs were established to honor their memory and ensure that the lessons of the Holocaust would not be forgotten.

In contemporary Amsterdam, the legacy of the Holocaust continues to shape the city's identity. The Jewish Historical Museum and the Anne Frank House serve as critical reminders of this history, fostering dialogue about tolerance, diversity, and the consequences of hatred. The impact of the Holocaust on Amsterdam's Jewish population is a powerful narrative of loss, resilience, and the enduring quest for remembrance and justice in the face of unimaginable tragedy.

Resistance and Collaboration

During the German occupation of Amsterdam from 1940 to 1945, the city became a focal point for both resistance movements and collaboration with the Nazi regime. The complexities of human behavior in times of oppression manifested through various actions taken by Amsterdam's citizens, ranging from heroic resistance to complicity with the occupying forces. The motivations behind these actions were diverse, influenced by personal beliefs, survival instincts, and the socio-political climate of the time.

Resistance Movements

As the Nazi regime implemented increasingly oppressive measures, including the deportation of Jews and the suppression of political dissent, a variety of resistance movements began to take form within Amsterdam. These groups comprised a mix of political activists, students, and ordinary citizens who sought to undermine the Nazi occupation through various means. One of the most notable resistance organizations was the "Amsterdamse Verzetsraad" (Amsterdam Resistance Council), which coordinated activities such as distributing underground newspapers, organizing strikes, and providing assistance to those in hiding.

The most famous act of resistance occurred on February 25, 1941, when a spontaneous protest against the deportation of Jews took place in Amsterdam. The protest, which saw thousands of citizens rallying against the persecution of the Jewish community, marked a significant moment of solidarity and defiance. However, the repercussions were severe, with the Nazi authorities retaliating by arresting and executing many involved, highlighting the grave risks associated with resistance.

In addition to organized groups, individual acts of bravery also characterized the resistance. Many citizens risked their lives to shelter Jewish neighbors and resist the Nazis' systematic efforts to round up the Jewish population. The efforts of figures like Anne Frank's family, who hid in a secret annex for two years, exemplify the personal sacrifices made by ordinary citizens to oppose tyranny.

Collaboration with the Nazis

In stark contrast to the resistance, some citizens chose to collaborate with the Nazis. This collaboration took various forms, from providing information on resistance activities to actively participating in the enforcement of Nazi policies. A significant faction of Dutch society, influenced by the political climate and the allure of power, aligned itself with the occupiers, believing that cooperation might yield benefits or mitigate the harshness of occupation.

Collaborators included members of the police and civil service who enforced Nazi decrees, such as the Aryanization of Jewish businesses. Some citizens viewed collaboration as a pragmatic choice in a desperate situation, believing that aligning with the occupiers might protect themselves and their families. Others, motivated by antisemitic sentiments or nationalistic fervor, saw collaboration as a way to bolster their ideological beliefs.

The Duality of Human Response

The duality of resistance and collaboration during the Nazi occupation in Amsterdam reflects broader themes of human behavior under duress. The choices made by citizens were often driven by a complex interplay of fear, moral conviction, and self-preservation. The consequences of these choices were profound and lasting, shaping post-war perceptions of guilt and complicity within Dutch society.

After the war, the narrative surrounding Amsterdam's response to the occupation was contentious. While some were celebrated as heroes, others faced ostracism or legal repercussions for their collaboration. The complexities of these experiences serve as a reminder of the moral ambiguities that arise in times of crisis.

In conclusion, the role of Amsterdam's citizens during the German occupation encompassed a spectrum of actions ranging from courageous resistance to willing collaboration. This period in Amsterdam's history exemplifies the challenging moral decisions individuals faced under oppressive regimes and highlights the enduring legacies of these choices in shaping collective memory and identity.

The Hunger Winter

The Hunger Winter of 1944-1945 stands as one of the darkest chapters in Amsterdam's history, a period marked by desperation, suffering, and resilience. As World War II raged on in Europe, the Netherlands found itself under Nazi occupation, which severely disrupted food supply lines and led to dire consequences for the civilian population. The combination of the German blockade, harsh winter conditions, and the economic exploitation of the occupied territories culminated in an unprecedented humanitarian crisis.

By the autumn of 1944, the situation in Amsterdam had become increasingly dire. The German authorities had implemented a series of measures that systematically restricted food and fuel supplies to the Dutch population. A major factor contributing to the Hunger Winter was the transportation strikes that took place in the summer of 1944, which the Nazis retaliated against by cutting off food supplies. The situation worsened as winter set in, with food rationing leading to severe shortages. Ration cards were issued, but the meager allowances provided were insufficient to sustain the population, particularly in urban areas where access to fresh produce was limited.

As the winter of 1944-45 unfolded, temperatures plummeted, and the city of Amsterdam was blanketed in snow. The cold exacerbated the already grim conditions, forcing families to seek warmth and sustenance in any way possible. Many were left to rely on makeshift heating solutions, often resulting in dangerous situations, as fuel became a luxury few could afford. The lack of adequate nutrition led to widespread malnutrition and illness, with many residents suffering from ailments such as tuberculosis and other respiratory diseases.

The community's response to the crisis showcased both the desperation and resourcefulness of the Amsterdam populace. Underground networks emerged, as families pooled resources, shared food, and organized soup kitchens to provide basic nourishment. Neighbors helped each other, often at great personal risk, while clandestine operations attempted to smuggle food into the city. The solidarity displayed among the citizens served as a poignant reminder of the human spirit's resilience in the face of adversity.

Despite these efforts, the toll of the Hunger Winter was devastating. Estimates suggest that around 20,000 people died as a direct result of starvation and related illnesses during this period in Amsterdam alone. The elderly and children were particularly vulnerable, and many families were irrevocably changed by the loss of loved ones. The psychological scars of this time would linger long after the war ended, leaving many to grapple with the memories of suffering and loss.

The end of the Hunger Winter came with the liberation of the Netherlands in May 1945, but the impact of this harrowing experience remained evident. The experiences of the Hunger Winter forced the Dutch society to confront issues of food security, health care, and community support systems, laying the groundwork for post-war recovery and the establishment of a welfare state. The trauma of this winter was inscribed into the collective memory of Amsterdam, becoming a cautionary tale about the consequences of war and occupation.

In summary, the Hunger Winter of 1944-45 was a catastrophic episode in Amsterdam's history that not only led to significant loss of life and suffering but also acted as a catalyst for societal change in the post-war era. The resilience of the people during this time highlighted the importance of community solidarity, and the lessons learned would shape the future policies of the Netherlands in addressing issues of social welfare and collective responsibility.

Liberation and Aftermath

The liberation of Amsterdam on May 5, 1945, marked a significant turning point in the city's history, concluding five years of Nazi occupation that had profoundly impacted its people, culture, and economy. The liberation was primarily orchestrated by Canadian troops, who faced sporadic resistance from German forces entrenched in the city. The moment of liberation was met with widespread jubilation among the citizens of Amsterdam, who had endured severe hardships, including the loss of life, food shortages, and the brutal repression of dissent. The streets were filled with celebratory crowds, as people waved flags and danced, expressing their relief and joy at the restoration of freedom.

However, the aftermath of liberation presented significant challenges. The immediate period following the city's liberation was marred by profound grief and loss. Amsterdam had seen the systematic extermination of a large portion of its Jewish population, with approximately 75% of the city's Jewish community perishing during the Holocaust. The emotional scars from this tragedy ran deep, leaving families shattered and communities devastated. Memorializing the victims became an essential aspect of the city's post-war identity, and the collective memory of loss would shape the cultural landscape for decades to come.

Economically, Amsterdam faced immense challenges post-liberation. The war had left the city's infrastructure in ruins, with buildings destroyed, factories damaged, and transportation systems severely impaired. The Dutch economy was in shambles, struggling to recover from the ravages of wartime devastation. Food shortages were rampant, and basic necessities were scarce. The population had to contend with the immediate effects of starvation and malnutrition, as rationing continued long after the war's end. The situation required urgent and coordinated efforts to stabilize the economy and restore essential services.

In the wake of the war, the Dutch government initiated a series of reconstruction programs aimed at revitalizing Amsterdam and the country at large. The Marshall Plan, initiated by the United States in 1948, played a crucial role in providing financial assistance to help rebuild war-torn Europe. Amsterdam benefited from this initiative, receiving essential funds that facilitated infrastructure repair, housing reconstruction, and the resumption of industrial production. The reconstruction efforts not only focused on physical rebuilding but also emphasized the importance of social cohesion and unity among the population, which had been fragmented during the war.

In addition to physical reconstruction, there was a significant shift in the political landscape of Amsterdam. The post-war period saw the rise of new political ideologies and movements advocating for social justice and equality. The war had exposed the vulnerabilities of the existing social order, leading to a reevaluation of policies and priorities. Labor unions gained strength, advocating for workers' rights and better living conditions, while the emergence of the welfare state began to take shape, laying the foundation for social policies that would define the Netherlands for decades.

Culturally, the liberation provided an impetus for a renaissance in the arts and intellectual life. Artists, writers, and musicians sought to express their experiences and emotions in the aftermath of the war. This cultural revival was characterized by a focus on themes of resilience, hope, and the human spirit's capacity to overcome adversity. The scars of war, while painful, became a source of inspiration for a generation of creators who were determined to rebuild not just the physical city but also its cultural identity.

In conclusion, the liberation of Amsterdam was a moment of profound significance that heralded the end of a dark chapter in the city's history. The challenges of post-war reconstruction were immense, but they also provided an opportunity for renewal. The efforts to rebuild the city, both physically and socially, laid the groundwork for a modern Amsterdam that embraced inclusivity, cultural richness, and resilience in the face of adversity. The legacy of this period continues to shape the city's identity and values, reflecting the enduring spirit of its people.

Chapter 7

Post-War Reconstruction and Growth

The Marshall Plan and Economic Recovery

After the devastation of World War II, Amsterdam, like many European cities, faced the daunting task of reconstruction and recovery. The city's infrastructure had been severely damaged during the war; buildings were destroyed, industries were crippled, and the economy was in shambles. In this context, the Marshall Plan, officially known as the European Recovery Program (ERP), became a pivotal factor in the revitalization of Amsterdam and the broader Dutch economy.

Launched in April 1948 by U.S. Secretary of State George C. Marshall, the plan aimed to provide substantial economic aid to European nations to help them rebuild after the war and to prevent the spread of communism by stabilizing economies. The Netherlands, being one of the countries most affected by the war, was one of the primary beneficiaries of this initiative. Over the course of the Marshall Plan, the Netherlands received approximately $1.5 billion in aid, which was instrumental in facilitating the country's recovery.

In Amsterdam, this influx of international aid had multifaceted impacts. Primarily, the financial resources provided through the Marshall Plan were channeled into rebuilding critical infrastructure. Essential services, such as transportation networks, communication systems, and utilities, were prioritized to restore functionality to the city. The reconstruction of the Amsterdam harbor, for example, was vital for re-establishing trade routes and ensuring that goods could flow into and out of the city efficiently. This not only supported local industries but also helped Amsterdam regain its status as a significant trading hub in Europe.

Moreover, the Marshall Plan facilitated the modernization of various sectors. The Dutch government, with the aid of American resources, began to implement industrial modernization programs. These programs encouraged the adoption of new technologies and practices that boosted productivity. Factories that had been repurposed during the war to produce munitions were now pivoted towards consumer goods, helping to meet the rising demand among the population. This shift not only created jobs but also revitalized the local economy, as new businesses emerged in response to changing consumer needs.

In addition to infrastructure and industrial support, the Marshall Plan emphasized the importance of social welfare. With the devastation of the war leading to increased unemployment and poverty, the Dutch government utilized Marshall funds to develop social programs. Initiatives aimed at improving housing conditions and providing social services were crucial in addressing the immediate needs of the population. The rebuilding of neighborhoods, which had been heavily bombed, was complemented by social housing projects that sought to ensure that all citizens had access to adequate living conditions.

Furthermore, the Marshall Plan also fostered international cooperation. The aid came with the expectation that recipient countries would work together to rebuild the European economy. In Amsterdam, this meant that local leaders were encouraged to engage with other municipalities in the Netherlands and beyond. The collaborative spirit engendered by the Marshall Plan led to the establishment of various regional and international partnerships that focused on economic development and cultural exchanges, strengthening Amsterdam's ties within the broader European context.

By the early 1950s, the impacts of the Marshall Plan were evident. Amsterdam experienced a remarkable economic recovery, marked by increased industrial output, improved living standards, and a revitalized infrastructure. The city began to emerge from the shadows of war, setting the stage for the economic boom of the 1960s and the development of the welfare state.

In conclusion, the Marshall Plan was not merely a financial aid program; it was a transformative force that catalyzed the recovery of Amsterdam's economy. Through the restoration of infrastructure, modernization of industry, enhancement of social welfare, and promotion of international cooperation, the plan laid the groundwork for a prosperous future, significantly altering the trajectory of Amsterdam and contributing to the overall stability of post-war Europe.

The Housing Crisis and New Urban Development in Amsterdam

The late 20th and early 21st centuries have seen Amsterdam grapple with a significant housing crisis, characterized by a sharp increase in demand for housing coupled with a shortage of available units. This crisis has its roots in several intertwined factors, including rapid urbanization, rising population density, and economic fluctuations that have transformed the city's housing landscape.

As the capital of the Netherlands, Amsterdam has consistently attracted individuals from across the globe, drawn by its vibrant culture, economic opportunities, and quality of life. Between the 1990s and the present, the city has experienced substantial population growth. The influx of international residents, students, and professionals has exacerbated the existing housing shortage, leading to soaring property prices and rents. The housing market has become increasingly competitive, with many locals struggling to find affordable housing. The situation became critical by the end of the 2010s, prompting urgent calls for action from residents, activists, and policymakers alike.

In response to the housing crisis, the city government has implemented a series of initiatives aimed at increasing the housing supply and addressing affordability issues. One of the key strategies has been the promotion of urban renewal projects in underdeveloped and historically neglected neighborhoods. The principle behind urban renewal is to revitalize these areas while preserving their unique character and enhancing livability. Projects often involve renovating existing buildings, introducing new residential developments, and improving public spaces.

A notable example of successful urban renewal is the transformation of the Eastern Docklands and the Westerdokseiland area. These former industrial zones have been reimagined as vibrant mixed-use neighborhoods, combining residential units with shops, cultural spaces, and recreational facilities. Through careful planning, the city has created attractive living environments that cater to diverse demographics, from young professionals to families.

Moreover, the city has prioritized the construction of social housing, a critical component in its efforts to ensure that all residents have access to affordable living options. This commitment is reflected in Amsterdam's housing policy, which mandates that at least 30% of new developments consist of social housing units. This approach aims not only to provide affordable options for lower-income residents but also to maintain social diversity within neighborhoods.

Additionally, the city has explored innovative housing solutions, such as cooperative housing models and temporary housing initiatives. These alternatives encourage community involvement and offer flexible living arrangements, often at lower costs. For instance, the temporary housing programs have been designed to accommodate refugees and those in urgent need while longer-term solutions are developed.

Sustainability has also become a focal point of new urban development in Amsterdam. The city has embraced green building practices and energy-efficient designs as part of its commitment to environmental stewardship. This includes initiatives to integrate green roofs, renewable energy sources, and sustainable drainage systems into new developments, which not only enhance the urban environment but also help mitigate the effects of climate change.

Despite these efforts, challenges remain. The balance between maintaining the city's historical character and accommodating modern demands is a delicate one, often leading to tensions between development and preservation. Furthermore, as Amsterdam continues to evolve, the risk of gentrification looms, threatening to displace long-standing communities and exacerbate social inequalities.

In conclusion, Amsterdam's housing crisis has prompted a multifaceted response involving urban renewal projects, a focus on affordable housing, innovative solutions, and a commitment to sustainability. While progress has been made, continuous efforts are necessary to ensure that the city remains inclusive and accessible for all its residents, preserving the unique character that makes Amsterdam a desirable place to live and work. The future of Amsterdam's housing landscape will hinge on the ability to navigate these complex challenges while fostering a vibrant and diverse urban environment.

Social Change and the Welfare State

The evolution of social policies and the welfare state in Amsterdam is a testament to the city's adaptive responses to changing social dynamics and economic conditions. The late 19th and early 20th centuries marked the beginning of significant reforms aimed at addressing the pressing issues of poverty, inequality, and industrialization's effects on the urban populace. The rapid urbanization during this period brought about a myriad of social challenges, necessitating a structured approach to welfare and social security.

The Seeds of Social Reform: Late 19th Century Context

In the late 1800s, Amsterdam experienced a notable demographic shift. The influx of rural populations into the city, drawn by industrial job opportunities, led to overcrowded living conditions and inadequate housing. Many residents faced dire poverty, a situation exacerbated by poor working conditions and limited access to healthcare. In response, early social reformers, influenced by socialist ideals and the burgeoning labor movement, began advocating for workers' rights and better living standards. This period saw the establishment of various charitable organizations aimed at providing support to the impoverished.

The Rise of the Welfare State: Early 20th Century Developments

The early 20th century heralded a more systematic approach to social welfare. The Dutch government, recognizing the need for comprehensive social policies, began implementing a series of reforms. The establishment of the Social Democratic Workers' Party (SDAP) in 1894 played a pivotal role in advocating for labor rights and social welfare. By 1919, after World War I, the principles of a welfare state began to crystallize, culminating in the introduction of social insurance programs, including health insurance and unemployment benefits.

Amsterdam, as the nation's economic hub, became a focal point for these developments. The city's local government actively participated in crafting policies aimed at alleviating poverty and enhancing the quality of life for its residents. Initiatives included the construction of public housing projects designed to provide affordable accommodation for the working class and the establishment of municipal health services.

Post-World War II Transformation: The Expansion of the Welfare State

The aftermath of World War II represented a turning point for Amsterdam's social policies. The devastation of the war and the subsequent economic challenges underscored the necessity for a robust welfare state. The Marshall Plan facilitated economic recovery, allowing Amsterdam to rebuild while simultaneously expanding its social safety nets.

By the 1950s, the welfare state in Amsterdam had evolved to encompass a wide array of social services, including comprehensive healthcare, education, and social housing. This expansion was characterized by a commitment to social equity and inclusion, reflecting the city's progressive values. The introduction of the Algemene Bijstandswet (General Assistance Act) in 1965 was a landmark moment, providing support for those unable to work, thereby reinforcing the state's responsibility towards its citizens.

Cultural Shifts and Social Movements: The 1960s and Beyond

The cultural upheaval of the 1960s, marked by the Provo movement and various social justice initiatives, further influenced Amsterdam's welfare policies. Grassroots activism led to increased awareness of issues such as gender equality, racial discrimination, and environmental concerns, prompting the city to address these emerging challenges within its social framework.

As Amsterdam continued to grapple with the complexities of modernization and globalization in the late 20th and early 21st centuries, the welfare state faced new challenges, including rising immigration and economic disparities. However, the city has remained committed to reinforcing its social policies, adapting them to ensure that all residents, regardless of background, have access to essential services and opportunities.

Conclusion

The development of the welfare state in Amsterdam is an ongoing narrative of social change, shaped by historical events, cultural shifts, and the persistent pursuit of equity and justice. As the city navigates contemporary challenges, its commitment to a comprehensive welfare system remains a cornerstone of its identity, reflecting the lessons learned from its past and the ongoing aspiration to foster a just and inclusive society.

The Rise of Tourism in Amsterdam

Amsterdam, with its picturesque canals, rich history, and vibrant cultural scene, has evolved into one of the world's most popular tourist destinations. The rise of tourism in Amsterdam can be traced through various socio-economic transformations, urban developments, and the city's strategic positioning within Europe.

Historical Context and Development

In the post-World War II era, particularly from the 1960s onwards, Amsterdam began to embrace its potential as a tourist destination. The city's recovery from the devastation of war coincided with a broader European trend of increasing mobility, as the rise of the middle class and advancements in transportation technology made travel more accessible. The establishment of international airlines, improvements in rail networks, and the advent of the automobile facilitated the influx of tourists eager to explore the city's unique charm.

Amsterdam's architectural beauty, characterized by its iconic canal houses and historic landmarks, played a critical role in attracting visitors. The restoration of historical sites and the promotion of cultural heritage became a priority for local authorities. In 1975, the city was recognized as a UNESCO World Heritage Site, which further spotlighted its cultural significance and made it a must-visit for tourists interested in history and architecture.

Cultural Attractions and Events

The city's rich cultural offerings have significantly contributed to its rise as a tourist hotspot. Amsterdam is home to world-class museums, including the Rijksmuseum, the Van Gogh Museum, and the Anne Frank House. Each of these institutions not only showcases remarkable collections but also draws millions of visitors annually, eager to experience the art and history that define the city.

Festivals and public celebrations also play a crucial role in enhancing Amsterdam's appeal. Events such as the King's Day celebrations, Amsterdam Dance Event, and the Amsterdam Light Festival attract both local residents and international tourists, creating a vibrant atmosphere that showcases the city's cultural diversity. These events have turned Amsterdam into a year-round destination rather than a seasonal one, providing a steady flow of visitors throughout the year.

Marketing and Promotion

The rise of tourism was also bolstered by targeted marketing strategies employed by the city's tourism board. Campaigns promoting Amsterdam's unique lifestyle, including its liberal policies on art, culture, and drugs, helped cultivate an image of the city as a progressive and open-minded destination. The "I Amsterdam" campaign, launched in the early 2000s, epitomized this effort, branding the city as a welcoming and inclusive place for all. This campaign not only highlighted key attractions but also encouraged visitors to explore lesser-known neighborhoods and experiences, thus dispersing tourism throughout the city.

Economic Impact and Urban Development

As tourism flourished, it significantly impacted Amsterdam's economy. The tourism sector became a vital source of employment, leading to the growth of hospitality, retail, and service industries. Hotels, restaurants, and local businesses thrived, contributing to the city's overall economic vitality.

However, the rapid rise of tourism has also brought challenges. Issues such as overcrowding, rising housing costs, and the gentrification of local neighborhoods have sparked debates about sustainable tourism practices. The city's administration has begun to implement measures aimed at balancing the needs of tourists with those of local residents, promoting responsible tourism and encouraging visitors to engage with the city beyond its most famous attractions.

Conclusion

Today, Amsterdam stands as a testament to the successful transformation of a city into a major international tourist destination. The interplay of historical significance, cultural richness, strategic marketing, and economic growth has positioned Amsterdam on the global tourism map. As the city continues to adapt to the changing dynamics of global travel, it remains committed to preserving its unique identity while embracing the opportunities that tourism brings. The future of Amsterdam as a tourist destination will hinge on its ability to navigate the complexities of sustainability and community engagement, ensuring that it remains a vibrant and welcoming place for generations to come.

Cultural Renaissance

The 1950s and 60s marked a pivotal period in Amsterdam's cultural history, characterized by a profound resurgence in artistic expression, social experimentation, and intellectual engagement. This cultural renaissance emerged in the wake of World War II, as the city began to recover from the trauma of occupation and the devastation wrought by conflict. The post-war environment fostered a sense of liberation and exploration, paving the way for significant transformations in art, music, literature, and social norms.

One of the defining features of this era was the emergence of a diverse artistic scene that sought to break free from traditional constraints. Artists and intellectuals were inspired by broader European movements, including Surrealism, Abstract Expressionism, and the burgeoning Beat Generation. The Dutch art scene became a melting pot of ideas, with Amsterdam serving as a hub for creative individuals who sought to challenge conventions and explore new forms of expression. This period saw the rise of influential groups and collectives, such as Cobra—an avant-garde movement that championed spontaneity and emotional expression in art. Founded in 1948 by artists from Copenhagen, Brussels, and Amsterdam, Cobra's impact reverberated throughout the city, as local artists embraced its ethos of creativity without borders.

The influence of counterculture movements during the 1960s further fueled Amsterdam's cultural revival. As global youth began to reject traditional societal norms, the city became a focal point for radical ideas and alternative lifestyles. The Provo movement, which emerged in the mid-1960s, epitomized this shift. The Provo activists sought to promote peace, love, and creativity, often using provocative performances and art installations to challenge authority and advocate for social change. Their antics, which included "white bicycles" as a symbol of free transportation and environmentalism, resonated with the city's youth and helped to foster a spirit of activism and engagement that would shape Amsterdam's cultural landscape for decades.

Musical innovation also played a significant role in this cultural renaissance. The rise of rock and roll, jazz, and folk music attracted a vibrant community of musicians and fans. Venues such as the Melkweg and Paradiso became hotspots for live performances, showcasing both local talent and international acts. The music scene in Amsterdam was not just about entertainment; it was intertwined with the broader countercultural movement, providing a platform for messages of peace, love, and social justice. Notable artists and bands emerged during this period, including the legendary Dutch rock band The Golden Earring, who would gain international fame.

Literature thrived as well, with Amsterdam becoming a nexus for writers who explored themes of identity, freedom, and societal critique. The city was home to influential literary figures like Harry Mulisch and Jan Wolkers, whose works delved into the complexities of post-war Dutch society. The growing acceptance of modernist literature and experimental writing reflected the changing attitudes of the populace, as readers sought new perspectives and narratives that challenged the status quo.

In addition to these artistic movements, the cultural renaissance of the 1950s and 60s also saw the emergence of diverse cultural institutions. Museums and galleries began to prioritize contemporary art, and public spaces were transformed into venues for artistic expression. The Stedelijk Museum, in particular, played a crucial role in showcasing modern and contemporary art, helping to solidify Amsterdam's reputation as a cultural capital.

In conclusion, the cultural renaissance of the 1950s and 60s in Amsterdam was marked by a flourishing of creativity and countercultural activism. Artists, musicians, and writers challenged traditional norms and explored new avenues of expression, shaping a vibrant cultural landscape that continues to influence the city today. This period not only revitalized Amsterdam's cultural identity but also laid the groundwork for the progressive, inclusive society that the city is known for in the modern era.

Chapter 8

The 1960s and 1970s - A Time of Change

The Provo Movement

The Provo Movement emerged in the 1960s as a significant countercultural phenomenon in Amsterdam, reflecting broader social and political changes occurring across Europe and the United States. This movement, characterized by its radical, anti-establishment ethos, sought to challenge the status quo and advocate for a more liberated and egalitarian society. Fueled by disillusionment with traditional values and authority, the Provos aimed to provoke thought and action through a blend of art, performance, and political activism.

At its core, the Provo Movement was born from a confluence of factors: the post-war economic boom, the rise of consumer culture, and the pervasive influence of American counterculture. Young people in Amsterdam, disenchanted with the rigid structures of the Dutch society, began to organize and express their frustrations. The movement found its voice in 1964 with the establishment of the Provo group, which originated as a response to urban issues, such as housing shortages and environmental degradation, exacerbated by rapid industrialization.

The Provos were known for their use of provocative and often playful tactics. One of their most famous acts was the "White Bicycle Plan," proposed in 1965, which aimed to provide free bicycles for public use, promoting a car-free, environmentally friendly mode of transportation. This initiative not only highlighted the need for sustainable urban development but also symbolized a rejection of consumerism and the automobile culture. Although the plan was never fully implemented, it demonstrated the Provos' innovative approach to activism and urban issues.

The Provos engaged in numerous public demonstrations and performances that blurred the lines between art and activism. Their events often involved a mix of humor, surrealism, and social critique, capturing public attention and encouraging participation. The group's antics, which included the distribution of leaflets and the staging of "protest performances," served to challenge societal norms and provoke discussions about freedom, equality, and the role of authority in everyday life. One of their notable actions included the symbolic "protest against the police," where they would mock law enforcement and highlight the increasing tensions between the youth and state authorities.

The impact of the Provo Movement extended beyond mere provocation; it played a crucial role in shaping Amsterdam's cultural landscape during the 1960s and 1970s. The movement inspired a wave of activism focused on various social issues, including civil rights, anti-war sentiment, and feminism. The Provo ethos of creativity and dissent influenced other movements and laid the groundwork for future activism in the city.

Moreover, the Provo Movement contributed to the broader zeitgeist of the 1960s, which emphasized individual freedom, self-expression, and social justice. It encouraged a re-evaluation of political and social structures, leading to significant changes in Dutch society. The ideals of the Provos found resonance in the burgeoning feminist movement, the anti-nuclear movement, and environmental activism, all of which sought to challenge existing power dynamics and promote progressive change.

Despite its relatively short-lived existence, the Provo Movement left a lasting legacy in Amsterdam. The movement catalyzed a cultural shift that embraced diversity, tolerance, and progressive values. It prompted discussions that would eventually lead to significant reforms in various social policies, including urban development, drug policy, and civil liberties. The Provos' spirit of countercultural activism continues to inspire new generations of activists in Amsterdam, reflecting the city's ongoing commitment to social justice and innovation.

In essence, the Provo Movement represents a pivotal moment in Amsterdam's history, where art and activism converged to challenge societal norms and advocate for a more equitable society. Its echoes are still felt today, as Amsterdam remains a vibrant hub for cultural expression and progressive thought, embodying the ideals that the Provos championed half a century ago.

Social Reforms and Civil Rights

Amsterdam has long been a crucible for social reform and civil rights movements, acting as a catalyst for progressive change not only within its own borders but also across the Netherlands and beyond. The city's unique socio-political landscape, characterized by a rich tapestry of cultures, traditions, and ideologies, has fostered an environment where social movements could thrive and challenge the status quo. This section explores the evolution of social reforms and civil rights in Amsterdam, highlighting key movements and the broader implications they had on society.

The late 19th and early 20th centuries marked a period of significant social upheaval in Amsterdam, driven largely by the rapid industrialization and urbanization that transformed the city. The rise of a working-class population led to widespread labor unrest, as workers sought better conditions, fair wages, and the right to unionize. Labor movements gained momentum throughout the 1880s and 1890s, culminating in the formation of the Dutch Trade Union Federation in 1905. Amsterdam became a focal point for strikes and demonstrations, with workers uniting to demand reforms that would improve their lives. These early labor movements laid the groundwork for subsequent social changes, as they not only empowered workers but also highlighted the need for comprehensive social welfare policies.

In the post-World War II era, Amsterdam witnessed the emergence of various social movements that sought to address issues of equality and justice. The women's rights movement gained traction during the 1960s, coinciding with global feminism. Activists in Amsterdam organized campaigns advocating for equal pay, reproductive rights, and an end to legal discrimination. The establishment of women's shelters and support networks provided vital resources for women facing domestic violence and social marginalization. The influence of these movements extended beyond Amsterdam, inspiring similar initiatives across the Netherlands and contributing to the eventual passage of landmark legislation, including the Equal Treatment Act of 1980.

The 1970s also saw the rise of the LGBTQ+ rights movement in Amsterdam, which played a pivotal role in advocating for the rights and acceptance of sexual minorities. The city's burgeoning counterculture provided a fertile ground for activism, culminating in the first Pride Parade in 1996, which celebrated love and diversity while demanding equal rights. Amsterdam's open-minded reputation attracted LGBTQ+ individuals from around the world, and the city has since become a global symbol of tolerance and acceptance. The legalization of same-sex marriage in the Netherlands in 2001 can be traced back to these grassroots movements in Amsterdam, which challenged societal norms and pushed for legislative change.

Moreover, the rise of multiculturalism in Amsterdam during the late 20th century brought about new civil rights discussions, particularly concerning the rights of immigrants and ethnic minorities. Activists and community organizations advocated for social integration, equal access to education, and anti-discrimination policies. The establishment of the "Stadsdeel" (district) councils allowed for greater representation of diverse communities within local governance, fostering a more inclusive political landscape.

Social movements in Amsterdam have not only been instrumental in shaping local policies but have also influenced national debates on social justice and civil rights. The activism that emerged within the city has reverberated through Dutch society, prompting reevaluations of laws and practices related to labor rights, gender equality, LGBTQ+ rights, and multiculturalism.

In conclusion, the social reforms and civil rights movements of Amsterdam have played a crucial role in influencing broader societal changes both within the Netherlands and internationally. The city's legacy of activism highlights the power of collective action and the ongoing struggle for equality, serving as a testament to the importance of advocacy in shaping a just society. As Amsterdam continues to evolve, these movements remind us of the need to remain vigilant in the pursuit of social justice for all.

Drug Culture and Policy in Amsterdam

Amsterdam is often perceived as a city with a liberal attitude towards drug use, a reputation that has evolved over decades. The development of Amsterdam's approach to drug use and policy reflects broader societal shifts and the city's unique historical context. This intricate relationship between culture, policy, and public perception has shaped Amsterdam into a focal point for discussions about drug legislation, public health, and social attitudes.

Historically, Amsterdam's approach to drugs began to shift in the 1960s, coinciding with global counterculture movements. The city became a hub for youth and artistic expression, attracting people drawn by its open-mindedness. This period saw the rise of soft drugs, particularly cannabis, which became increasingly normalized within the social fabric of the city. The establishment of "coffeeshops" in the 1970s marked a significant turning point; these establishments allowed for the legal sale and consumption of cannabis under regulated conditions. The rationale was to distinguish between soft and hard drugs, thereby focusing law enforcement efforts on more dangerous substances while creating a controlled environment for cannabis users.

The policy of tolerance, or "gedoogbeleid," emerged as a cornerstone of the Dutch approach to drug use. This policy is characterized by a pragmatic acknowledgment of drug use as a reality rather than a purely criminal issue. By allowing certain forms of drug use and possession within specific limits, the government aimed not only to reduce the harm associated with drug use but also to divert resources away from policing to public health initiatives. This approach was largely successful in keeping drug-related crime rates relatively low compared to other cities worldwide.

Throughout the 1980s and 1990s, however, Amsterdam faced challenges related to drug use, particularly with the increase in hard drugs such as heroin and cocaine. The rise of drug-related crime and public health crises, including HIV/AIDS among intravenous drug users, prompted a reevaluation of the existing policies. In response, the city implemented harm reduction strategies, which included needle exchange programs, supervised consumption rooms, and extensive outreach efforts aimed at educating the public about safer drug use practices. These initiatives were designed to minimize health risks and reduce the stigma associated with addiction, fostering a more compassionate societal attitude towards drug users.

As the 21st century approached, the landscape of drug policy in Amsterdam continued to evolve. The city grappled with the complex realities of globalization and increasing tourism, which brought about new challenges such as drug tourism. The influx of international visitors seeking to experience Amsterdam's liberal drug culture led to concerns about public safety, health, and the overall quality of life for residents. In response, local authorities began to impose stricter regulations on coffeeshops, including limitations on their numbers and the introduction of residence requirements for customers.

Amsterdam's approach to drug policy is not without its critics. Proponents of stricter drug laws argue that the city's permissive stance may encourage drug use among youth and exacerbate public health issues. Conversely, advocates for the current policies maintain that a harm reduction approach is essential for addressing the complexities of drug addiction and that criminalization only serves to perpetuate cycles of stigma and violence.

In recent years, the conversation around drug policy in Amsterdam has also included discussions about decriminalization and legalization. As debates continue globally around these issues, Amsterdam remains at the forefront of innovative approaches to drug use, balancing public health, safety, and individual freedoms. The city's evolving drug culture and policy illustrate a unique case study in how societal attitudes can shape legislative frameworks, reflecting broader trends in public health and social justice around the world.

The Women's Movement

The women's movement in Amsterdam has a rich and multifaceted history, significantly shaping both the city's social fabric and the broader landscape of women's rights in the Netherlands. During the late 19th and early 20th centuries, as in many parts of the world, women in Amsterdam began to mobilize for their rights, driven by the burgeoning awareness of gender inequality and the desire for social reform. This period marked the emergence of various feminist groups that sought to address issues such as suffrage, education, labor rights, and reproductive rights.

In the early 1900s, the women's suffrage movement gained momentum, with activists organizing rallies, petitions, and public discussions to advocate for voting rights. One of the pivotal organizations was the Dutch Women's Union (Nederlandsche Vrouwenbond), established in 1889, which played a crucial role in uniting women across various social strata to fight for their rights. The suffrage movement in Amsterdam was characterized by a coalition of women from diverse backgrounds, including middle-class activists, working-class women, and intellectuals, all seeking to challenge the patriarchal structures that limited their participation in political and social life.

The struggle for women's suffrage reached a significant milestone in 1919 when women in the Netherlands finally gained the right to vote, following years of persistent advocacy. This achievement not only empowered women politically but also inspired future generations to continue fighting for gender equality. The impact of this success resonated throughout Amsterdam, as women began to assume more prominent roles in public life, including in politics, education, and the workforce.

The interwar period saw the rise of second-wave feminism, with a focus on broader social issues such as workplace equality, reproductive rights, and social justice. In Amsterdam, women's rights activists increasingly addressed the intersectionality of gender with class, race, and sexuality, recognizing that the fight for women's rights could not be separated from other social justice movements. Organizations like the Women's Action Committee emerged, advocating for equal pay, maternity leave, and access to contraception. Their efforts laid the groundwork for significant policy changes in the post-World War II era.

The 1960s and 1970s marked a notable turning point in the women's movement, influenced by global feminist movements and the counterculture of the time. Activists in Amsterdam organized protests and campaigns that challenged traditional gender roles and sought to raise public awareness about issues such as domestic violence and sexual harassment. The establishment of women's shelters and crisis centers became a priority, addressing the urgent needs of women facing violence and discrimination.

The feminist movement in Amsterdam also embraced cultural expression as a means of activism. Women artists, writers, and performers used their platforms to challenge societal norms and advocate for women's rights. The emergence of feminist literature and art contributed to a growing cultural dialogue about gender equality, making visible the struggles and achievements of women in society.

As the movement evolved, it encountered new challenges in the late 20th and early 21st centuries, including the rise of multiculturalism and the need to address the rights of migrant women. Activists in Amsterdam recognized the importance of inclusivity within the feminist movement, advocating for the rights of all women, regardless of their background or identity.

Today, Amsterdam continues to be a center for feminist activism, with organizations like Women Inc. and The Netherlands Women's Council working tirelessly to address ongoing issues such as gender-based violence, workplace discrimination, and reproductive rights. The legacy of the women's movement in Amsterdam serves as a testament to the power of collective action and the enduring struggle for gender equality, inspiring future generations to continue the fight for justice and equity in all spheres of life.

Economic Challenges and Innovation in Amsterdam

As Amsterdam transitioned through the 20th century, it faced a series of economic challenges that tested the city's resilience and adaptability. The aftermath of World War I, the Great Depression of the 1930s, and the subsequent shifts in global economic paradigms all posed significant hurdles. However, Amsterdam's response to these challenges exemplified a blend of innovation and strategic planning, allowing the city to emerge as a dynamic hub for economic activity.

Post-World War I Recovery

Following World War I, Amsterdam, like many European cities, grappled with economic instability. The war had disrupted trade routes and caused significant damage to infrastructure, leading to high unemployment and housing shortages. The city's recovery was partly facilitated by the Marshall Plan after World War II, which injected much-needed capital into the Dutch economy and stimulated reconstruction efforts. This financial assistance enabled Amsterdam to rebuild its damaged infrastructure, including transportation systems that were crucial for both trade and mobility.

The Great Depression

The Great Depression posed a profound challenge for Amsterdam in the 1930s. As global markets contracted, the city experienced a sharp decline in trade and industry. Unemployment rates soared, and social unrest grew as citizens demanded solutions from their government. In response, the city initiated public works programs, which not only provided employment but also improved urban infrastructure. This period saw the construction of new roads, bridges, and housing, laying the groundwork for future economic resilience.

Post-War Industrialization and Innovation

The post-war period marked a significant shift in Amsterdam's economic landscape. With the decline of traditional industries, such as shipping and fishing, the city began to diversify its economy. The rise of technology and the service sector became key drivers of growth. Amsterdam embraced innovation, fostering an environment conducive to new business ventures and technological advancements. Initiatives to promote entrepreneurship emerged, with a focus on sectors such as finance, information technology, and creative industries.

The establishment of the Amsterdam Science Park in the late 20th century epitomized this focus on innovation. This research hub brought together academia, industry, and government, facilitating collaboration and the commercialization of new technologies. Amsterdam also became a center for startups, particularly in the tech sector, which attracted talent and investment from across the globe.

Navigating Economic Liberalization

The late 20th century saw the rise of neoliberal economic policies, which emphasized deregulation, privatization, and free markets. While these changes initially led to economic uncertainty, Amsterdam adeptly navigated this transformation by embracing its role as a global financial center. The city's strategic location and advanced infrastructure positioned it as a vital entry point for international trade, particularly within Europe.

The financial sector flourished, with Amsterdam becoming a hub for banking and investment services. The city's stock exchange, one of the oldest in the world, adapted to the changing economic landscape by modernizing its operations and incorporating technological advancements. This adaptability ensured that Amsterdam remained competitive in a rapidly evolving global economy.

Conclusion

The economic challenges facing Amsterdam throughout the 20th century catalyzed significant transformation within the city. By leveraging innovation, embracing diversification, and fostering a culture of entrepreneurship, Amsterdam not only weathered economic downturns but also emerged as a vibrant and resilient economic center. The lessons learned during these tumultuous periods continue to inform the city's approach to contemporary challenges, ensuring that Amsterdam remains at the forefront of economic innovation and development in the 21st century.

Chapter 9

Amsterdam in the 1980s and 1990s

Economic Liberalization

The 1980s and 1990s marked a transformative phase in Amsterdam's economic landscape, characterized by the adoption of neoliberal policies that reshaped the city's economic and social structure. Economic liberalization, which emphasizes free markets, deregulation, and reduced state intervention, played a pivotal role in this transformation, influencing various aspects of life in Amsterdam.

At the core of these neoliberal policies was the belief that a free-market economy would spur growth and innovation. The Dutch government, responding to the global economic climate and pressures from international financial institutions, began to shift its approach. This shift involved privatization of state-owned enterprises, deregulation of labor markets, and a focus on attracting foreign investment. Amsterdam, as the economic heart of the Netherlands, was at the forefront of this transition.

One significant consequence of economic liberalization was the rise of the service sector. As traditional manufacturing industries faced stiff competition from abroad, there was a marked shift toward services, technology, and finance. Amsterdam became a hub for multinational corporations, financial institutions, and tech startups, bolstering its reputation as a global financial center. The establishment of the Amsterdam Stock Exchange as a leading financial marketplace highlighted the city's growing importance in international finance. This transformation not only created a plethora of job opportunities but also attracted a diverse workforce from around the world, enhancing Amsterdam's multicultural character.

However, while economic liberalization spurred growth, it also led to significant social changes and challenges. The deregulation of the housing market, for example, resulted in increased real estate speculation, driving up property prices and rents. Many long-standing residents found it increasingly difficult to afford housing, contributing to a growing divide between the affluent and economically disadvantaged. This phenomenon was particularly evident in neighborhoods undergoing gentrification, where new developments catered to wealthier residents, displacing lower-income communities and altering the social fabric of these areas.

In addition to housing challenges, the shift towards a neoliberal economy also affected labor relations and social policies. The weakening of labor unions, which had traditionally played a strong role in securing workers' rights and benefits, led to increased job insecurity and a rise in temporary employment contracts. The gig economy began to take shape during this period, with many workers facing precarious employment conditions and limited access to social protections. As a result, social inequalities became more pronounced, with marginalized groups, including immigrants and low-skilled workers, experiencing heightened vulnerability.

Moreover, the focus on economic growth often came at the expense of social welfare programs. As the government prioritized fiscal austerity and reduced public spending, many social services faced budget cuts. This shift raised concerns about the welfare state's ability to support its most vulnerable citizens, leading to increased advocacy for social justice and equity.

Despite these challenges, economic liberalization also fostered a spirit of entrepreneurship and innovation. The city became home to numerous startups and creative industries, particularly in technology, design, and culture. Amsterdam's vibrant cultural scene thrived during this period, with the city embracing its identity as a center for artistic expression and creativity, further attracting talent and tourism.

In summary, the economic liberalization of the late 20th century profoundly impacted Amsterdam's economy and social structure. While it catalyzed growth and innovation, it also exacerbated social inequalities and housing challenges. The city's response to these dual realities continues to shape its policies and initiatives as it strives for a balanced approach to growth that considers both economic prosperity and social equity.

The Housing Market Boom

The housing market boom in Amsterdam during the late 20th century and early 21st century marked a significant transformation in the city's urban landscape, social fabric, and economic dynamics. This period was characterized by a surge in real estate speculation, rapid development, and a growing demand for housing, driven by factors such as increasing immigration, globalization, and a burgeoning service sector. Understanding the intricate interplay of these elements provides insight into the complexities of Amsterdam's housing market and the resulting socio-economic implications.

The late 1980s and early 1990s initiated a shift as Amsterdam began to experience an influx of international businesses and expatriates, attracted by the city's strategic position as a financial and cultural hub. This influx led to a rising demand for housing, particularly in desirable neighborhoods. As a result, property values started to climb, encouraging developers to invest in new residential projects. The city's planning policies evolved to accommodate this growth, often favoring large-scale developments that promised to meet the burgeoning demand for housing.

However, alongside genuine demand, speculation began to take root within the real estate market. Investors, both domestic and international, saw Amsterdam's increasing popularity as an opportunity for financial gain. The rise of buy-to-let investments became prevalent, with properties being purchased not for residency but as rental investments. This trend intensified competition for available housing, driving prices even higher and leading to the gentrification of previously affordable neighborhoods. Areas such as the Jordaan and De Pijp, once home to working-class families, began to witness a transformation as wealthier residents moved in, attracted by the charm and amenities these areas offered.

The impact of real estate speculation was profound, as it exacerbated the housing crisis in Amsterdam. Many long-term residents found themselves priced out of their own neighborhoods, leading to social tensions and a sense of displacement among communities. The rental market became increasingly competitive, with landlords capitalizing on the high demand by raising rents. Consequently, many residents faced housing insecurity, as affordability became a pressing issue in a city known for its high quality of life.

In response to mounting concerns over housing affordability and availability, the municipal government implemented measures aimed at curbing speculation and protecting vulnerable populations. Policies included rent controls, regulations on short-term rentals (such as those facilitated by platforms like Airbnb), and initiatives to promote social housing. The city sought to balance the interests of investors while ensuring that a diverse range of housing options remained accessible to all residents.

Despite these interventions, the housing market boom left an indelible mark on Amsterdam's urban landscape. New architectural developments reshaped the city's skyline, with modern residential complexes juxtaposing traditional canal houses. This shift not only altered the physical appearance of the city but also its demographic makeup, as an influx of international residents brought diverse cultural influences, enriching the social tapestry of Amsterdam.

As the 21st century progressed, the housing market continued to evolve, reflecting broader economic trends and societal shifts. The challenges of affordability and access to housing remained central to discussions about urban policy and social equity. The ongoing dialogue about the housing market in Amsterdam serves as a microcosm of the global struggle between economic development and social justice, highlighting the need for sustainable and inclusive urban planning.

In conclusion, the housing market boom in Amsterdam illustrates the complex relationship between real estate speculation, urban development, and social dynamics. As the city navigates the future, the lessons learned from this period will be crucial in shaping policies that foster a balanced and equitable housing landscape for all its residents.

Immigration and Multiculturalism

Amsterdam has long been a city characterized by its openness and diversity, stemming from its historical role as a thriving trade hub and a center for commerce and culture. As globalization accelerated during the late 20th century, the dynamics of immigration intensified, bringing new waves of migrants from various regions around the world. This influx has profoundly shaped Amsterdam's cultural landscape, contributing to a rich tapestry of multicultural influences that define the city today.

During the 1980s and 1990s, Amsterdam experienced significant immigration from countries in the former Yugoslavia, Turkey, Morocco, and Suriname, among others. These new communities brought with them distinct languages, customs, and culinary traditions, enriching the city's cultural mosaic. For instance, Turkish and Moroccan migrants introduced their vibrant culinary practices, leading to the proliferation of restaurants and markets offering traditional dishes such as kebabs, couscous, and tagines. This culinary diversity not only broadened the gastronomic options available to residents and tourists but also fostered intercultural exchanges that enhanced social cohesion.

The presence of these diverse communities has also influenced Amsterdam's artistic and cultural production. The city has become a canvas for multicultural expression, where art forms such as hip-hop, contemporary dance, and theater often reflect the experiences and narratives of immigrant populations. Festivals celebrating cultural heritage, such as the Keti Koti Festival, which commemorates the abolition of slavery, have gained prominence, emphasizing the contributions of Afro-Surinamese culture to the Dutch identity. Similarly, events like the Amsterdam Dance Event showcase the international music scene, drawing on influences from various immigrant communities.

The impact of immigration extends beyond cultural contributions; it has also led to significant changes in the demographic makeup of the city. Amsterdam's neighborhoods, particularly in areas like De Pijp and Oost, have transformed into vibrant multicultural hubs. These neighborhoods are characterized by a mix of traditional Dutch architecture alongside shops, markets, and community centers reflecting diverse heritages. The resulting cultural blend has made Amsterdam an appealing destination for both locals and tourists seeking authentic experiences.

However, the increase in immigration has not come without challenges. Issues of integration, social cohesion, and sometimes tension have emerged, particularly in the context of economic disparities and the rise of nationalist sentiments. The city's political landscape has seen the emergence of parties advocating for stricter immigration policies, often fueled by concerns over identity and social cohesion. In response, grassroots initiatives and organizations dedicated to promoting intercultural dialogue and understanding have sprung up, aiming to bridge divides and foster inclusivity.

Education has played a critical role in addressing the challenges posed by immigration. Schools in Amsterdam have become increasingly multicultural, often reflecting the diversity of the city's population. Educational initiatives focused on multicultural education have been implemented to promote understanding and respect among students from different backgrounds. These efforts not only enhance the learning experience but also cultivate a sense of belonging and community among young people.

In conclusion, the impact of increased immigration on Amsterdam's cultural landscape is multifaceted, shaping the city's identity as a global metropolis. While it has enriched the cultural fabric through diversity in cuisine, art, and community life, it has also presented challenges that demand thoughtful engagement and policy responses. As Amsterdam continues to evolve in the 21st century, embracing its multicultural identity will be crucial in fostering unity and resilience in the face of ongoing global changes. This legacy of diversity positions Amsterdam not only as a beacon of tolerance and inclusivity but also as a model for other cities navigating the complexities of immigration and multiculturalism in a globalized world.

The Growth of the Service Sector in Amsterdam

As Amsterdam transitioned into the late 20th century, the city witnessed a significant transformation in its economic landscape, characterized by a marked shift from an industrial economy to a service-based one. This transformation was not merely a response to global economic trends; it was also a product of local conditions, strategic decisions, and the unique characteristics that define Amsterdam.

In the post-World War II period, Amsterdam's economy was heavily reliant on traditional industries, such as shipping, textiles, and manufacturing. However, by the 1980s, the global economy was evolving rapidly, driven by advancements in technology, globalization, and a growing emphasis on information and services. In response to these changes, Amsterdam began to reposition itself as a center for service-oriented industries, which included finance, tourism, technology, and creative sectors.

One of the most significant catalysts for this shift was the rise of the financial services sector. Amsterdam had long been a hub for trade and commerce, but the establishment of the Amsterdam Stock Exchange (the oldest stock exchange in the world) laid the groundwork for a burgeoning financial services industry. This sector attracted both domestic and international investment, fostering a climate of innovation and entrepreneurship. By the late 20th century, Amsterdam had cemented its status as a leading financial center in Europe, with a concentration of banks, investment firms, and insurance companies that contributed significantly to the city's economic output.

In parallel, the city's strategic location as a gateway to Europe facilitated the growth of logistics and distribution services. The Port of Amsterdam, one of the largest ports in Europe, evolved to meet the demands of global trade, while the development of Schiphol Airport further enhanced Amsterdam's connectivity. This logistical prowess allowed service industries to flourish, supporting a vast array of businesses reliant on efficient supply chains and transportation networks.

Tourism also played a vital role in the growth of Amsterdam's service sector. The city's rich cultural heritage, iconic architecture, and vibrant arts scene made it an attractive destination for millions of visitors each year. The establishment of cultural institutions, such as the Rijksmuseum and the Van Gogh Museum, along with annual events and festivals, contributed to a booming tourism industry. This influx of tourists not only generated economic activity but also led to the development of hospitality, retail, and entertainment sectors, all of which became critical components of the service economy.

Moreover, the rise of the technology sector in Amsterdam became a defining feature of the city's economic transformation. In the late 1990s and early 2000s, the city began to attract tech startups and digital companies, spurred by a vibrant ecosystem of innovation, investment, and talent. Initiatives such as the Amsterdam Innovation Motor and the establishment of tech hubs and incubators catalyzed this growth, positioning Amsterdam as a leading European tech hub. The focus on technology and digital services created new job opportunities and attracted a diverse workforce, further diversifying the service sector.

Social changes also contributed to this economic evolution. The demand for more flexible work arrangements, leisure activities, and lifestyle services reflected shifting consumer preferences. As people sought experiences over material goods, businesses adapted by offering services that catered to this new mindset, including co-working spaces, wellness services, and experiential dining.

In conclusion, Amsterdam's shift from an industrial economy to a service-based one is a multifaceted transformation influenced by global trends, local initiatives, and changing societal needs. This evolution not only reshaped the economic landscape of Amsterdam but also reinforced its position as a cosmopolitan city, rich in culture and innovation. As the city continues to adapt to new challenges and opportunities, the growth of the service sector remains a cornerstone of its economic identity.

Cultural and Artistic Developments in Amsterdam during the 1980s and 1990s

The 1980s and 1990s marked a significant period of cultural and artistic evolution for Amsterdam, characterized by the emergence of new institutions and movements that reflected the city's dynamic socio-political landscape. This era was defined not only by the remnants of post-war reconstruction but also by a burgeoning sense of identity and experimentation in the arts.

Emergence of New Cultural Institutions

During this time, Amsterdam witnessed the establishment and expansion of various cultural institutions that would play pivotal roles in shaping the city's artistic identity. The Stedelijk Museum, a museum dedicated to modern and contemporary art and design, underwent significant renovations and expansions in the late 20th century, enhancing its profile as a leading institution for avant-garde art. This revitalization allowed for the exhibition of international contemporary artists alongside Dutch talents, fostering a rich dialogue between local and global artistic practices.

In addition to established institutions, smaller, independent galleries and art spaces began to emerge, particularly in neighborhoods like the Jordaan and Oud-West. These venues provided platforms for young and experimental artists, contributing to a vibrant grassroots art scene. Collectives such as The Amsterdam Art Foundation and De Appel became instrumental in promoting contemporary art through exhibitions, performances, and artist residencies, emphasizing the importance of community engagement and innovative practices.

Artistic Movements and Trends

The 1980s also saw the rise of new artistic movements that challenged traditional forms and boundaries. Postmodernism gained traction, influencing artists to explore themes of identity, culture, and societal critique. This led to a proliferation of mixed media, installation art, and performance art, which often addressed pressing social issues such as gender, race, and environmental concerns.

Artists like Marlene Dumas and Rineke Dijkstra emerged during this period, gaining recognition for their explorative approaches to portraiture and the human condition. Their works resonated with the public, prompting discussions around representation and the complexities of identity in a rapidly changing world. The influence of street art also became prominent, with artists like The London Police and Delta making their marks on the urban landscape, turning Amsterdam's streets into open-air galleries and engaging the community in artistic expression.

The Role of Music and Performance

In parallel with visual arts, the music scene flourished during the 1980s and 1990s, reflecting Amsterdam's cultural diversity and progressive ethos. The city became a hub for various music genres, including electronic music, punk, and hip-hop. Venues such as Melkweg and Paradiso became iconic spaces for live performances, showcasing both local talent and international acts.

The Dutch Festival of Theatre, established in this era, further highlighted the importance of performing arts, bringing together innovative theater companies and fostering collaborations that pushed the boundaries of traditional storytelling. These performances often addressed contemporary issues, serving as a mirror to Amsterdam's evolving societal landscape.

Cultural Renaissance and Global Influence

Overall, the cultural and artistic developments of the 1980s and 1990s in Amsterdam were marked by a spirit of experimentation and inclusivity. The city not only embraced its historical artistic legacy but also opened its arms to global influences, creating a melting pot of ideas and expressions. This renaissance laid the groundwork for Amsterdam to emerge as a vibrant cultural capital, influencing artistic movements worldwide and establishing a framework for future generations of artists. As the city navigated the complexities of globalization, the lessons learned during this transformative period would continue to resonate, shaping Amsterdam's identity as a hub of creativity and innovation in the years to come.

Chapter 10

The New Millennium

Amsterdam in a Globalized World

As we entered the 21st century, Amsterdam emerged as a vibrant microcosm of globalization, reflecting and responding to the profound changes brought about by the interconnectedness of the global economy, culture, and demographics. This transformation has led to significant shifts in various aspects of the city, from economic practices to cultural expressions, ultimately reshaping its identity.

Economic Impact of Globalization

The economic landscape of Amsterdam has undergone a dramatic transformation due to globalization. Traditionally a trading hub since its inception, the city has leveraged its historical advantages—such as its strategic location and extensive port facilities—while adapting to the demands of a globalized economy. The rise of digital technology and the internet has spurred Amsterdam's evolution into a key player in the tech industry. The city has attracted numerous startups and tech companies, solidifying its status as a European tech hub. The presence of innovative spaces like the Amsterdam Science Park and the burgeoning startup ecosystem has fostered economic growth and diversification, positioning the city as a center for knowledge-based industries.

Moreover, the financial sector has also thrived, with Amsterdam being home to major banks, investment firms, and insurance companies that have expanded their reach globally. The establishment of the Amsterdam International Financial Centre (AIFC) has further bolstered the city's reputation as a leading financial center, providing a conducive environment for international business and finance.

Cultural Influence and Exchange

Culturally, globalization has invigorated Amsterdam's dynamic arts scene, fostering an environment of cross-cultural exchange. The city's rich heritage—encompassing its historical landmarks, museums, and artistic traditions—has been complemented by an influx of diverse cultural influences brought in by immigrants and international residents. This has resulted in a vibrant cultural mosaic where traditional Dutch art coexists with influences from various global cultures.

Art institutions such as the Rijksmuseum and the Van Gogh Museum continue to celebrate the Dutch Masters while also hosting exhibitions that showcase contemporary global artists, reflecting the city's embrace of international art trends. Festivals such as the Amsterdam Dance Event and the International Documentary Film Festival Amsterdam (IDFA) attract global audiences and artists, further enriching the city's cultural fabric.

Furthermore, the culinary scene in Amsterdam has experienced a renaissance, with a plethora of international restaurants and food markets emerging. This gastronomic diversity not only enhances the city's appeal as a tourist destination but also fosters cultural exchange and understanding among its residents.

Demographic Shifts

Demographically, globalization has transformed Amsterdam into a melting pot of cultures. The city has seen an increase in immigration, with individuals from various backgrounds contributing to its growth and vibrancy. This demographic shift has brought about a rich blend of languages, traditions, and lifestyles, making Amsterdam one of the most multicultural cities in Europe.

The integration of diverse communities is evident in neighborhoods such as De Pijp and Amsterdam-Noord, where various cultures coexist, contributing to the city's unique character. However, this diversity also brings challenges, such as social cohesion and inclusion. Therefore, Amsterdam has made concerted efforts to address these challenges through social policies aimed at promoting integration and fostering a sense of belonging among all residents.

In conclusion, globalization has significantly impacted Amsterdam, enhancing its economic prospects, cultural richness, and demographic diversity. As the city continues to navigate the complexities of a globalized world, it stands as a testament to how local identities can thrive amidst global influences, shaping a future that is both inclusive and dynamic. The interplay of tradition and modernity will undoubtedly continue to define Amsterdam as it moves forward in an increasingly interconnected world.

Sustainability and Urban Planning

Amsterdam has positioned itself as a global leader in sustainable urban development, a reputation forged through innovative policies, ambitious projects, and the active engagement of its citizens. As one of the most densely populated cities in Europe, Amsterdam faces unique challenges, including housing shortages, traffic congestion, and environmental degradation. In response, the city has adopted a multifaceted approach to urban planning that prioritizes sustainability, resilience, and quality of life.

One of the cornerstones of Amsterdam's sustainable urban development strategy is its commitment to reducing carbon emissions. The city has set ambitious goals to become carbon-neutral by 2050, with intermediate targets for 2025. Key to this effort is the promotion of renewable energy sources, particularly solar and wind power. The city's rooftops are increasingly adorned with solar panels, and wind turbines have been installed both onshore and offshore. The municipal government has incentivized energy efficiency renovations in residential and commercial buildings, encouraging the use of sustainable materials and energy-saving technologies.

Public transportation plays a vital role in Amsterdam's sustainability efforts. The city has invested heavily in expanding and modernizing its public transport network, including tram, bus, and metro systems, to reduce reliance on private vehicles. Moreover, Amsterdam is renowned for its cycling culture, with an extensive network of bike lanes that make cycling a safe and convenient option for residents. The municipal government promotes cycling through bike-sharing programs and initiatives aimed at improving bike parking and security. These efforts not only reduce traffic congestion but also enhance air quality, contributing to the overall health of the urban environment.

Urban green spaces are another critical aspect of Amsterdam's sustainable planning. The city has prioritized the creation and maintenance of parks, community gardens, and green roofs, which help to mitigate urban heat, improve biodiversity, and provide residents with access to nature. Projects like the "Green Roof Initiative" encourage property owners to transform their roofs into green spaces, which provide insulation, manage stormwater, and create habitats for wildlife. The city's commitment to green infrastructure reflects a holistic understanding of urban ecology, recognizing the interdependence between people and the environment.

Amsterdam's approach to urban planning also emphasizes social sustainability. The city actively engages its citizens in the planning process, ensuring that the voices of diverse communities are heard and considered. Initiatives like "Participatory Urban Planning" allow residents to contribute ideas and feedback on new developments, fostering a sense of ownership and investment in their neighborhoods. This participatory model not only enhances the quality of urban design but also strengthens social cohesion and community resilience.

Moreover, Amsterdam has embraced the circular economy concept, aiming to minimize waste and maximize resource efficiency. The city has established ambitious waste management goals, including a target to recycle 65% of its waste by 2025. Initiatives such as "Amsterdam Circular 2020" promote practices like composting, reusing materials, and supporting businesses that prioritize circularity in their operations. The city's commitment to reducing waste aligns with its broader sustainability goals, creating a more resilient urban ecosystem.

In conclusion, Amsterdam's efforts in sustainable urban planning reflect a comprehensive and forward-thinking approach to addressing the challenges of urbanization. By prioritizing renewable energy, enhancing public transportation, fostering green spaces, engaging citizens, and embracing circular economy principles, Amsterdam is setting a benchmark for cities worldwide. As the city navigates the complexities of the 21st century, its commitment to sustainability will be vital in ensuring a vibrant, livable, and resilient urban environment for future generations.

Technological Innovation

In the early 21st century, Amsterdam emerged as a prominent center for technological innovation, gaining recognition as a leading tech hub and smart city. This transformation was driven by a combination of factors, including a vibrant startup culture, supportive governmental policies, and a highly educated workforce. The city's strategic location in Europe, coupled with its advanced digital infrastructure, positioned it as an attractive destination for tech companies and entrepreneurs alike.

One of the key elements that facilitated Amsterdam's rise as a tech hub was its robust startup ecosystem. The city is home to numerous incubators, accelerators, and co-working spaces that foster innovation and collaboration among entrepreneurs. Organizations such as StartupAmsterdam and the Amsterdam Economic Board have played pivotal roles in nurturing the startup scene, offering resources, mentorship, and networking opportunities. This supportive environment has led to the emergence of several successful tech companies, including Adyen, Booking.com, and TomTom, which have made significant contributions to both the local and global economies.

Moreover, Amsterdam's commitment to becoming a smart city has propelled its technological advancements. The municipality has actively invested in smart infrastructure projects that integrate digital technology into urban management and service delivery. Initiatives such as smart traffic management systems, energy-efficient street lighting, and intelligent waste management have improved the quality of life for residents while promoting sustainability. The city's focus on innovation in public transport, which includes the integration of apps for real-time travel information, exemplifies Amsterdam's approach to enhancing urban mobility through technology.

The city has also established itself as a leader in the field of sustainability, leveraging technology to address environmental challenges. Amsterdam's "Green Deal" program encourages businesses to adopt sustainable practices, and the city's commitment to reducing carbon emissions aligns with its technological initiatives. The development of smart grids and renewable energy projects showcases Amsterdam's dedication to creating a greener urban environment. Additionally, the city's extensive bicycle infrastructure, supported by digital applications for bike-sharing and navigation, highlights the blend of technology and sustainability in Amsterdam's urban planning.

Education and research play crucial roles in Amsterdam's technological landscape. The presence of prestigious universities and research institutions, such as the University of Amsterdam and the Vrije Universiteit, provides a steady stream of talent and innovative ideas. These institutions collaborate with the tech industry to drive research and development, fostering an environment of continuous learning and adaptation. Furthermore, Amsterdam hosts various tech-focused events and conferences, such as The Next Web Conference, which attracts global attention and encourages knowledge sharing among industry experts, entrepreneurs, and investors.

The city's commitment to inclusivity and diversity has also contributed to its success as a tech hub. Amsterdam has cultivated a multicultural environment that embraces talent from around the world, enriching its innovation landscape. Initiatives aimed at increasing diversity in tech, such as Women in Tech and various programs promoting underrepresented groups, have created a more equitable industry. This inclusivity not only fosters creativity but also enhances Amsterdam's reputation as a welcoming city for tech talent.

As Amsterdam continues to evolve in the digital age, its focus on technological innovation has positioned it as a model for smart cities globally. The integration of technology into everyday life, along with a commitment to sustainability, education, and inclusivity, has created a vibrant urban ecosystem that thrives on innovation. Looking ahead, Amsterdam's ability to adapt to emerging technologies and trends will be essential in maintaining its status as a leading tech hub and smart city, shaping not only its future but also serving as an inspiration for cities around the world.

Social Policy and Inclusion in Amsterdam

Amsterdam, known for its rich history and vibrant multiculturalism, has long been a city that grapples with the challenges and opportunities of social inclusion and inequality. The city's approach to these issues has evolved over the years, shaped by historical events, shifting demographics, and changing political ideologies. Today, Amsterdam is characterized by a commitment to social policies aimed at fostering inclusivity and addressing the disparities that exist within its diverse population.

Historical Context and Policy Development

The foundations of Amsterdam's social policy can be traced back to the post-World War II era when the Netherlands experienced rapid urbanization and economic growth. This period saw the establishment of a welfare state that prioritized social security, housing, education, and healthcare. However, as the city grew, so did the complexities of its social fabric. The influx of immigrants and refugees, particularly from former colonies and war-torn regions, added layers of cultural diversity but also highlighted inequalities in access to resources and opportunities.

In the late 20th century, Amsterdam began adopting more targeted social policies to address the needs of marginalized groups. The city government recognized that economic growth alone would not eliminate social disparities. Programs aimed at improving housing conditions, enhancing educational opportunities, and providing employment support for disadvantaged groups became central to the city's agenda.

Current Initiatives for Inclusion

Today, Amsterdam's social policy framework is articulated through a combination of municipal strategies and local initiatives. One of the key pillars is the "Amsterdam Inclusion Agenda," which aims to promote social equality across various sectors, including employment, education, health, and housing. This comprehensive approach involves collaboration between local government, non-profit organizations, community groups, and the private sector.

The city has invested in initiatives that target specific populations facing social exclusion, such as immigrants, the homeless, and low-income families. For instance, the "Talent Development Program" focuses on integrating young immigrants into the labor market by providing vocational training, language courses, and mentorship opportunities. This program not only assists individuals in finding meaningful employment but also fosters social cohesion by promoting interaction among diverse communities.

Additionally, Amsterdam has prioritized affordable housing to combat the rising cost of living and prevent gentrification, which disproportionately affects lower-income residents. The city has set ambitious targets for constructing social and affordable housing units, with policies that encourage mixed-income neighborhoods. This strategy aims to create inclusive communities where people from various socio-economic backgrounds can coexist.

Community Engagement and Empowerment

An essential aspect of Amsterdam's approach to social inclusion is community engagement. The city actively involves residents in decision-making processes related to social policies, ensuring that the voices of marginalized groups are heard and considered. Community councils and participatory budgeting initiatives allow citizens to influence how resources are allocated, fostering a sense of ownership and agency among residents.

Moreover, local organizations play a crucial role in advocating for the rights of underrepresented groups. Grassroots movements and NGOs work tirelessly to highlight issues of inequality and push for systemic change, whether in education, employment, or public services. These organizations often serve as intermediaries, connecting marginalized communities with the resources and support they need.

Challenges and the Path Forward

Despite these efforts, Amsterdam still faces significant challenges related to social inclusion and inequality. Disparities in educational attainment, employment rates, and access to healthcare persist, particularly among ethnic minorities and low-income families. The COVID-19 pandemic further exacerbated these issues, highlighting the vulnerabilities of marginalized populations.

To address these ongoing challenges, Amsterdam's government continues to adapt and refine its social policies, focusing on innovation and evidence-based strategies. By fostering an inclusive environment that values diversity and promotes equal opportunities, Amsterdam aims not only to improve the lives of its residents but also to serve as a model for other cities grappling with similar social issues. The city's commitment to social policy and inclusion reflects a broader understanding that true prosperity is only achievable when all citizens can participate fully in society.

The Future of Amsterdam

As Amsterdam stands at the threshold of a new era, the city faces a unique intersection of challenges and opportunities that will shape its trajectory in the coming decades. This dynamic urban environment, known for its rich history and cultural significance, is now tasked with navigating the complexities of globalization, technological advancements, and social changes, all while striving to maintain its identity and quality of life for its residents.

One of the foremost challenges confronting Amsterdam is the ongoing housing crisis. Rapid population growth, combined with an influx of international migrants and expatriates, has strained the housing market, leading to skyrocketing rents and a shortage of affordable housing. As the city seeks to accommodate its growing population, innovative housing solutions will need to be explored. This might include the development of sustainable housing projects, repurposing underutilized spaces, and implementing policies that promote inclusive housing strategies. Balancing the need for new developments with the preservation of Amsterdam's architectural heritage will be crucial in maintaining the city's unique character.

Another significant challenge lies in the realm of sustainability. Amsterdam has garnered a reputation as a leader in sustainable urban development, but the city must continue to evolve in response to climate change and environmental degradation. Initiatives aimed at reducing carbon emissions, enhancing public transportation, and promoting green spaces will be vital.

The city's commitment to sustainability must also extend to its economy, with a focus on fostering green industries and encouraging circular economy models that minimize waste. The integration of smart technologies in urban planning can further enhance efficiency and sustainability, making Amsterdam a model for other cities worldwide.

Technological innovation presents both a challenge and an opportunity for Amsterdam. As the city positions itself as a tech hub, issues related to data privacy, cybersecurity, and the digital divide must be addressed. Ensuring that all residents have access to digital resources and skills is essential for fostering an inclusive society. Moreover, the rise of automation and artificial intelligence could disrupt traditional employment sectors, necessitating proactive measures in education and workforce development. Fostering partnerships between educational institutions, businesses, and government bodies will be critical in preparing the workforce for future demands.

Social inclusivity is another area where Amsterdam will need to focus its efforts. The city is characterized by its multicultural population, which enriches its cultural fabric but also presents challenges in terms of social cohesion. Addressing issues of inequality, discrimination, and integration will require concerted efforts from policymakers, community leaders, and residents alike. Initiatives aimed at promoting cultural understanding and fostering community engagement can help bridge divides and strengthen social ties.

Furthermore, Amsterdam's role in international relations is poised for evolution. As global dynamics shift, the city must navigate its position within the European Union and its relationships with other global cities. The ongoing discourse surrounding climate change, migration, and trade will require Amsterdam to assert itself as a leader in collaborative efforts addressing these pressing issues. Enhancing diplomatic relations and participating in international organizations can amplify the city's influence on the global stage.

In conclusion, the future of Amsterdam is a tapestry woven with both challenges and opportunities. By embracing innovative solutions, prioritizing sustainability, fostering inclusivity, and reinforcing its global connections, Amsterdam can not only preserve its historical legacy but also carve out a path toward a vibrant and resilient future. As the city continues to evolve, its ability to adapt to changing circumstances will be key in shaping an Amsterdam that remains a beacon of culture, innovation, and social harmony in the years to come.

Chapter 11

Amsterdam's Architectural Heritage

Medieval and Renaissance Architecture

Amsterdam's architectural heritage is a testament to its rich history, reflecting the city's evolution from a modest fishing village to a bustling metropolis. The medieval and Renaissance periods were particularly formative, laying the groundwork for the distinctive architectural identity that characterizes Amsterdam today. This section explores the oldest buildings and architectural styles from these pivotal eras, shedding light on how they shaped the city's urban landscape.

Medieval Beginnings

The origins of Amsterdam can be traced back to the late 12th century, with the establishment of a dam along the Amstel River. The earliest structures in the city were primarily utilitarian, built to serve the needs of its inhabitants. The medieval architecture of Amsterdam was predominantly influenced by the Romanesque style, characterized by its thick walls, rounded arches, and solid construction. One of the earliest surviving examples of medieval architecture is the Oude Kerk (Old Church), consecrated in 1306. This Gothic edifice, with its stunning wooden ceiling and intricate stained glass, represents the transition from Romanesque to Gothic architecture, showcasing the city's growing wealth and devotion.

In addition to religious buildings, Amsterdam's medieval architecture included merchant houses and guildhalls, constructed from brick to reflect both durability and prosperity. The Waag (Weighhouse), built in the late 15th century, exemplifies this style. Originally a weighing station for goods, its striking Gothic features, including pointed arches and decorative gables, highlight the importance of trade in Amsterdam's early development.

The Renaissance Influence

By the 16th century, the Renaissance began to influence Amsterdam's architectural style, introducing elements of classical antiquity. This period marked a shift towards symmetry, proportion, and the use of columns and pilasters in building designs. The Nieuwe Kerk (New Church), completed in 1665, is a prime example of Renaissance architecture, with its grand façade and harmonious proportions. The church's towering spire, reaching 85 meters, is a significant landmark in Amsterdam's skyline, symbolizing the city's growing prominence.

During this time, the rise of the merchant class led to the construction of opulent townhouses that reflected the wealth of their owners. The Canal Ring, developed in the 17th century, is a UNESCO World Heritage site that showcases the architectural styles of the period. The canals lined with iconic gabled houses, often three to five stories high, exhibit a blend of Renaissance influences and the Dutch Gothic style, characterized by their stepped gables and intricate brickwork. These houses were not just residences; they were statements of status, with many featuring ornate facades adorned with carved stone and decorative motifs.

Architectural Legacy

The architectural styles of the medieval and Renaissance periods laid the foundation for Amsterdam's future developments. The integration of Gothic elements with Renaissance principles created a unique architectural dialogue that can still be observed in the city today. Buildings from these periods not only serve as historical landmarks but also as cultural symbols, reflecting the city's identity and evolution.

As Amsterdam moved into the Baroque period and beyond, the legacy of its medieval and Renaissance architecture remained influential. The aesthetic appreciation for brick as a primary building material continued, and the architectural innovations of these early periods paved the way for modern interpretations.

In conclusion, the medieval and Renaissance architecture of Amsterdam encapsulates the city's historical narrative, revealing its transformation through time. The oldest buildings, with their artistic craftsmanship and historical significance, continue to inspire and inform Amsterdam's architectural ethos, standing as enduring monuments to its rich cultural heritage.

The Canal Ring

The Canal Ring, or Grachtengordel, is one of Amsterdam's most distinctive and recognizable features, embodying the city's historical and architectural essence. Constructed in the early 17th century during the Dutch Golden Age, this elaborate network of canals was designed to facilitate urban expansion and provide a means of transportation and defense. The layout reflects meticulous urban planning that harmonizes functionality with aesthetic appeal, making it a UNESCO World Heritage Site in 2010.

Origins and Development

The genesis of the Canal Ring can be traced back to the burgeoning population and the economic prosperity of Amsterdam in the late 16th and early 17th centuries. As the city transformed into a major trading hub, the need for additional land became paramount. The city planners, led by the visionary architect Hendrick de Keyser, sought to create a systematic and organized urban environment that would accommodate the influx of merchants and their wealth. The three primary canals—Herengracht, Prinsengracht, and Keizersgracht—were excavated, each lined with grand townhouses and warehouses, and designed to facilitate shipping and trade.

The construction of the Canal Ring was not just a practical solution to urban overcrowding but also a statement of wealth and power. The houses built along the canals, known as grachtenhuizen, showcased the affluence of their owners, featuring ornate gables, large windows, and intricate facades. The architectural styles of these canal houses varied from Renaissance to Baroque, illustrating the eclectic tastes of the era. Many of these houses were designed with a narrow width to maximize the number of properties that could be built along the limited waterfront.

Architectural Significance
The architecture of the canal houses is significant, not only for its beauty but also for its reflection of social stratification and urban organization. The wealthier merchants and civic leaders inhabited the larger, more elaborately decorated houses on the Herengracht, while the more modest townhouses on the Prinsengracht catered to the middle class. This stratification of housing along the canals illustrates Amsterdam's social hierarchy, with the layout promoting both exclusivity and community.

Moreover, the innovative use of space in these narrow houses, often extending deep into the block, allowed for functional living arrangements, including spacious interiors and elaborate gardens at the rear. The design of these homes often included large windows and high ceilings, fostering a sense of grandeur and light, which was in stark contrast to the cramped conditions found in other European cities of the time.

Cultural Impact
The Canal Ring is not merely an architectural marvel; it is also a cultural symbol of Amsterdam. The canals played a crucial role in the socio-economic life of the city; they facilitated trade, transportation, and communication, contributing to Amsterdam's status as a global trading power. The waterway network allowed for the movement of goods and people, linking the city to international markets and enhancing its economic clout.

Today, the Canal Ring continues to be a vibrant heart of Amsterdam, attracting millions of tourists each year. This UNESCO World Heritage Site remains a testament to the ingenuity and vision of 17th-century planners, encapsulating the spirit of the Dutch Golden Age. The canals are not only a picturesque backdrop for the city's cultural and social activities but also serve as a reminder of Amsterdam's rich history and its enduring legacy in urban design.

In conclusion, the Canal Ring, with its iconic canal houses and structured layout, stands as a symbol of Amsterdam's historical significance, architectural innovation, and cultural vitality. It reflects the city's evolution from a modest settlement to a bustling metropolis, showcasing the interplay between urban planning and societal development. As Amsterdam continues to grow and evolve, the Canal Ring remains a cherished and vital part of its identity.

Art Deco and Modernism

The early 20th century marked a significant turning point in architectural design, as the world moved towards modernity, and Amsterdam was no exception to this transformative wave. The emergence of Art Deco and Modernism during this period introduced new aesthetics, materials, and philosophies that would permanently alter the fabric of the city's architecture.

The Art Deco Movement

Art Deco, characterized by its bold geometric patterns, vibrant colors, and lavish ornamentation, emerged in the 1920s as a response to the austere designs of the preceding era. In Amsterdam, this style flourished in both public and private buildings, reflecting the city's growing affluence and desire for modernity. One of the most notable examples of Art Deco architecture in Amsterdam is the Ziggurat-shaped Haarlemmerpoort, built in 1912, which showcased the angular forms and decorative flourishes typical of the style.

The Art Deco movement also found expression in the residential architecture of the time. The Amsterdam School, a Dutch architectural movement that began in the early 20th century, heavily influenced Art Deco design in the city. Its architects, such as Michel de Klerk, combined traditional forms with modern materials, creating buildings that were both functional and artistically rich. The Zaanstraat complex and Haveneiland developments stand as testaments to this era, featuring intricate brickwork and stylized decorative motifs that echo the Art Deco ethos.

The Rise of Modernism

As the 1920s progressed, Modernism began to dominate the architectural landscape. This movement emphasized simplicity, functionality, and a break from historical styles, favoring clean lines and open spaces. Amsterdam's transition towards Modernism was epitomized by the construction of the Amsterdam School of Architecture, which advocated for a rational approach to design that prioritized utility and social welfare.

One of the most iconic examples of Modernist architecture in Amsterdam is the Van Nelle Factory, completed in 1931. Designed by architects Bruno Taut and Willem van den Broek, this building is celebrated for its innovative use of glass and steel, allowing for abundant natural light and creating an airy, open environment for workers. The factory's design not only represented a significant industrial advancement but also embodied the Modernist belief in the power of architecture to enhance productivity and improve quality of life.

Integration with Urban Planning
The influence of Art Deco and Modernism extended beyond individual buildings; it also impacted urban planning in Amsterdam. The Plan Zuid, conceived by architect Hendrik Petrus Berlage in the early 20th century, was an ambitious urban development project that sought to integrate green spaces, residential areas, and commercial hubs. This plan incorporated elements of Modernism, promoting a balanced relationship between architecture and the urban environment. The resulting neighborhoods, such as Zuid and De Pijp, exemplified the ideals of Modernist urbanism, featuring wide streets, ample parks, and functional public spaces.

Cultural Impact and Legacy
Art Deco and Modernism not only transformed Amsterdam's architectural landscape but also reflected broader societal changes. These styles emerged during a time of economic prosperity and cultural experimentation, paralleling shifts in lifestyle and values. The emphasis on functionality and social responsibility inherent in Modernist design resonated with the growing movement towards social reform and improved living conditions for all citizens.

Today, the legacy of Art Deco and Modernism is evident in Amsterdam's diverse cityscape. The interplay of these architectural styles has created a unique urban environment that marries historical richness with modern innovation, making Amsterdam a living museum of architectural evolution. The continued preservation and appreciation of these styles highlight their importance in understanding the city's historical narrative and cultural identity. As Amsterdam navigates contemporary challenges, the lessons learned from the Art Deco and Modernist movements remind us of the power of architecture to shape society and foster community.

Post-War Architecture
The aftermath of World War II brought profound changes to Amsterdam's architectural landscape. The destruction wrought by the war, coupled with the pressing need for housing and infrastructure, catalyzed a transformative period characterized by a departure from pre-war architectural styles and a pursuit of modernism. This evolution not only addressed the immediate post-war needs but also reflected broader social, economic, and cultural shifts in Dutch society.

In the immediate years following the war, Amsterdam faced a severe housing crisis. The war had left many buildings damaged or destroyed, and returning soldiers and displaced citizens created an urgent demand for homes. To tackle this challenge, the city embraced a pragmatic approach, prioritizing functionality and efficiency over stylistic concerns. The result was a wave of utilitarian architecture, marked by simple, straightforward designs that often utilized prefabricated materials. These structures, while lacking in aesthetic complexity, provided essential shelter and reflected the economic realities of the time.

As the 1950s progressed, a shift began to emerge in architectural philosophy, influenced by the broader European trends of modernism. This period saw the introduction of the International Style, characterized by clean lines, open spaces, and the use of glass and steel. Prominent architects such as Aldo van Eyck and Hugo Alvar Henrik Aalto began to experiment with these principles, integrating them into their designs for public buildings, schools, and residential complexes. Van Eyck's designs, especially, emphasized human scale and community engagement, moving away from the monolithic structures of the past to create more inviting environments.

The 1960s brought a wave of innovative architectural projects that sought to redefine urban living. The construction of the Bijlmermeer, a large-scale housing development in the southern part of the city, epitomized the ideals of modernist urban planning. Designed by architects including H.P. Berlage, the complex was characterized by its high-rise buildings set amidst green spaces, aiming to create a self-sufficient community. However, the realities of social integration and urban decay in the Bijlmermeer later highlighted the shortcomings of such utopian projects, leading to critiques of modernist ideals.

In the 1970s and 1980s, Amsterdam's architecture began to reflect a growing awareness of social issues and the importance of context in urban design. The city embraced a more eclectic architectural philosophy, as seen in the work of architects like Herman Hertzberger. His designs emphasized flexibility and the importance of public spaces, fostering interaction among residents. This period also saw the rise of postmodern architecture, which celebrated historical references and local character, contrasting sharply with the stripped-down modernism of previous decades.

By the late 20th century, Amsterdam's architectural landscape had evolved to embrace sustainability and innovation. The 1990s and early 2000s witnessed a rise in environmentally conscious design, as architects sought to integrate green technologies and sustainable practices into their work. Projects like the Amsterdam ArenA and the renovation of the city's historic waterfront reflected this trend, blending modern design with the city's rich architectural heritage.

Today, Amsterdam continues to balance its historical identity with contemporary innovation. The city's commitment to sustainability is evident in projects such as the Zuidas district, which combines modern office spaces with green technology, and the revival of traditional neighborhoods through adaptive reuse of older buildings. This ongoing evolution of architectural styles not only shapes the physical environment of Amsterdam but also influences its cultural and social fabric, making the city a living testament to the interplay between history and modernity.

In conclusion, the evolution of post-war architecture in Amsterdam reflects a dynamic response to the challenges of its time, marked by a balance of practicality, community engagement, and an ongoing commitment to sustainability. This rich architectural heritage continues to inform the city's identity and offers valuable lessons for urban development in the contemporary world.

Contemporary Architecture

In recent decades, Amsterdam has experienced a dynamic evolution in its architectural landscape, characterized by a blend of innovation, sustainability, and respect for historical context. Contemporary architecture in Amsterdam reflects the city's commitment to embracing modern design while addressing pressing social and environmental challenges. This period of architectural development has seen the introduction of groundbreaking projects that not only transform the urban fabric but also redefine the relationship between the built environment and its inhabitants.

One of the most prominent aspects of contemporary architecture in Amsterdam is the city's commitment to sustainability. As climate change poses significant threats to urban areas worldwide, Amsterdam has positioned itself as a leader in sustainable urban development. Architects and urban planners have increasingly integrated eco-friendly materials and energy-efficient technologies into their designs. Notable examples include the The Edge, an office building completed in 2014 that boasts a variety of sustainable features, including solar panels, green roofs, and smart technology systems that optimize energy consumption. The building's innovative design won accolades for its environmentally conscious approach and set a benchmark for future developments.

Moreover, the city's urban planning emphasizes the importance of green spaces and public areas. Projects like the Amsterdam North Docklands highlight the integration of recreational areas within new urban developments. This waterfront area, previously an industrial site, has transformed into a vibrant community that combines residential buildings, cultural venues, and ample green spaces, creating an inviting atmosphere for residents and visitors alike. This shift towards human-centric design reflects a broader trend in contemporary architecture that prioritizes livability and community engagement.

Another significant trend within Amsterdam's contemporary architectural movement is the adaptive reuse of historical buildings. Rather than demolishing older structures, architects are increasingly repurposing them to serve modern functions. This practice not only preserves the historical character of the city but also reduces the environmental impact of new construction. The Amsterdam Central Library (OBA), for instance, is a striking example of how modern design can complement historical elements. The library occupies a former industrial site and features a sleek, modern aesthetic that harmonizes with its surroundings while providing a crucial cultural resource for the community.

Furthermore, contemporary architecture in Amsterdam is marked by a growing emphasis on innovation and experimentation. Architectural firms are exploring new materials, forms, and technologies, leading to unique and striking designs that challenge conventional notions of space and functionality. The A'DAM Tower, a renovated 20th-century office building turned entertainment hub, exemplifies this spirit of innovation. It features a rooftop observation deck with panoramic views of the city and is home to various cultural and recreational spaces, highlighting the blend of commercial, creative, and community-focused elements in modern Amsterdam.

The city's commitment to inclusivity is also reflected in its contemporary architecture. Projects like the Bijlmerbajes, a former prison converted into a mixed-use neighborhood, showcase how architectural design can foster social cohesion and diversity. This redevelopment emphasizes affordable housing, community facilities, and public spaces, promoting a sense of belonging among residents from various backgrounds.

In conclusion, contemporary architecture in Amsterdam is a vibrant tapestry woven from threads of sustainability, innovation, and inclusivity. The city's approach to modern design not only enhances its aesthetic appeal but also addresses critical social and environmental issues, positioning Amsterdam as a forward-thinking urban center. As the city continues to evolve, its architectural landscape will undoubtedly reflect its rich history while paving the way for a sustainable and inclusive future.

Chapter 12

Amsterdam's Cultural Influence

The Dutch Masters and Amsterdam

The city of Amsterdam, known for its picturesque canals and vibrant atmosphere, has long been a pivotal center for art and culture, particularly during the Golden Age of the 17th century. It was during this period that artists such as Rembrandt van Rijn and Vincent van Gogh emerged, leaving indelible marks on the city's cultural identity and on the broader canvas of art history. Their works not only reflect the artistic innovations of their times but also encapsulate the spirit, social norms, and philosophical undercurrents of Dutch society.

Rembrandt van Rijn: The Master of Light and Shadow

Rembrandt, born in 1606, is often heralded as one of the greatest painters in Western art history. He chose Amsterdam as his home and studio, where he produced a staggering body of work, including portraits, landscapes, and historical scenes. His innovative use of chiaroscuro—the technique of using strong contrasts between light and dark—revolutionized portrait painting and allowed him to convey deep emotional narratives. Works such as "The Night Watch" not only showcase his mastery of technique but also reflect the themes of civic pride and collective identity that resonated with the citizens of Amsterdam during its Golden Age.

Amsterdam's burgeoning wealth and influential status during this time provided Rembrandt with a diverse clientele, from prosperous merchants to city officials, which enabled him to capture the essence of Dutch society. His portraits often depicted subjects with remarkable realism, conveying individuality and emotional depth, thus elevating the genre from mere representation to a profound exploration of human experience. Rembrandt's legacy in Amsterdam is not confined to his paintings; his approach to art influenced generations, instilling a sense of pride in Dutch artistic achievement that remains a key aspect of the city's cultural identity.

Vincent van Gogh: The Voice of Emotion and Innovation

Fast forward to the late 19th century, and we encounter Vincent van Gogh, whose life and work further shaped Amsterdam's cultural narrative. Although Van Gogh was not born in Amsterdam, his time spent in the city was significant for both his personal development and for the broader art movements of the period. Van Gogh's stay in Amsterdam, particularly during his formative years, exposed him to the works of the Dutch Masters, which greatly influenced his artistic style.

Van Gogh's use of vibrant colors and expressive brushwork broke away from traditional artistic conventions, paving the way for modern art movements such as Expressionism and Post-Impressionism. His iconic works—such as "The Starry Night" and "Sunflowers"—are characterized by a passionate exploration of color and emotion that resonates with viewers to this day. Although he struggled with mental health issues and faced considerable adversity during his life, Van Gogh's posthumous fame and the establishment of the Van Gogh Museum in Amsterdam solidified his place in the pantheon of great artists, further enhancing the city's cultural cachet.

Cultural Identity and Legacy

The impact of artists like Rembrandt and Van Gogh extends beyond their individual contributions. They have become emblematic of Amsterdam's rich artistic heritage, reflecting the city's evolution through the lenses of different historical contexts. The works of these masters are not only housed in prestigious institutions like the Rijksmuseum and the Van Gogh Museum but also serve as cultural touchstones that connect Amsterdam's past with its present.

The legacy of the Dutch Masters is interwoven into the fabric of Amsterdam's identity, influencing not only the visual arts but also literature, theater, and contemporary cultural expressions. Their stories resonate with the ideals of creativity, resilience, and innovation that continue to define Amsterdam as a vibrant cultural capital. As the city navigates the complexities of modernity, the enduring influence of Rembrandt and Van Gogh reminds us of the profound power of art to shape cultural identity and foster a sense of community within the ever-evolving narrative of Amsterdam.

The Role of Amsterdam in Literature

Amsterdam has long been a fertile ground for literary creativity, serving as both a backdrop and a character in a multitude of works that reflect not only the city's cultural richness but also the broader human experience. The city has influenced Dutch literature profoundly, and its impact has resonated across international literary landscapes.

Historical Context

The literary scene in Amsterdam began to flourish during the Renaissance, when the city emerged as a hub for art, philosophy, and humanism. The publication of texts in the Dutch language became more prominent, driven by the city's role as a center for printing and publishing. The flourishing of the printing press allowed works by writers such as Joost van den

Vondel and P.C. Hooft to reach wider audiences. Vondel, often referred to as the "Dutch Shakespeare," produced plays and poetry that not only showcased the complexities of human nature but also reflected the socio-political climate of 17th-century Amsterdam.

The Dutch Masters and Their Influence

In the 19th and 20th centuries, as Amsterdam solidified its reputation as a cultural capital, its influence extended into modern literature. Authors such as Multatuli (Eduard Douwes Dekker) used Amsterdam as a backdrop to critique colonialism and social injustices in his seminal work "Max Havelaar." This book not only brought attention to the plight of the Javanese people under Dutch colonial rule but also sparked a broader discussion on ethics and responsibility in literature.

Similarly, the works of writers like Harry Mulisch and Cees Nooteboom reflect the existential concerns of post-war Europe, often intertwining personal narratives with the historical context of Amsterdam. Mulisch's "The Assault" explores themes of guilt, memory, and the impact of World War II on individual lives, while Nooteboom's prose often captures the city's intricate relationship with time and existence.

Amsterdam as a Literary Setting

The city itself has frequently appeared as a canvas in literary works, embodying the complexities of urban life. Amsterdam's canals, narrow streets, and vibrant neighborhoods provide a rich tapestry for storytelling. The famous "Anne Frank: The Diary of a Young Girl" not only chronicles the harrowing experiences of a Jewish girl hiding during the Nazi occupation but also portrays the city's historical significance during one of humanity's darkest chapters. Frank's poignant observations and reflections highlight the duality of Amsterdam as a place of beauty and a site of profound suffering.

Moreover, contemporary authors like Arnon Grunberg and Esther Gerritsen continue to explore Amsterdam's multifaceted identity through their narratives. Grunberg's works often delve into themes of alienation and modernity, reflecting the complexities of life in a rapidly changing city. Gerritsen, on the other hand, examines the nuances of human relationships against the backdrop of Amsterdam's urban landscape, often blending humor with poignant social commentary.

A Global Literary Hub

Amsterdam's role as a cosmopolitan city has further enhanced its literary significance. The city hosts various international literary festivals, such as the Amsterdam International Literature Festival, which provides a platform for authors from around the globe. This exchange of ideas fosters a dynamic literary culture that transcends national boundaries, making Amsterdam a nexus for literary dialogue and innovation.

In conclusion, Amsterdam's influence on literature is both profound and multifaceted. From its rich historical context to its vibrant contemporary literary scene, the city has shaped the works of numerous authors and continues to serve as a source of inspiration. As a setting, a character, and a catalyst for literary exploration, Amsterdam remains an indelible part of the literary canon, inviting readers to engage with its stories for generations to come.

Music and Performing Arts

Amsterdam has long been a vibrant hub for music and performing arts, reflecting the city's rich cultural tapestry and historical evolution. From its early days as a trading port to its present status as a cosmopolitan capital, the development of music and theater in Amsterdam has been influenced by various social, political, and cultural dynamics.

Historical Roots and Early Influences

The origins of Amsterdam's music scene can be traced back to the late medieval period when the city began to flourish as a center of trade. This prosperity allowed for the patronage of musicians and composers, fostering an environment rich in artistic expression. The 16th and 17th centuries, particularly during the Dutch Golden Age, saw a significant growth in musical activity, with the establishment of various guilds and organizations that supported musicians.

The Reformation and subsequent conflicts had a profound impact on religious music, shaping the musical landscape of the time. The rise of the Protestant Church led to the emergence of new forms of worship music, while Catholic influences persisted, leading to a blend of styles that characterized the period. Composers such as Jan Pieterszoon Sweelinck emerged during this time, whose works laid the groundwork for future generations.

Theatrical Developments

Theater in Amsterdam also has deep historical roots, with the first permanent theater, the Amsterdamse Schouwburg, established in 1637. This venue became a focal point for drama and performance arts, showcasing both local and international works. The theater scene flourished, attracting playwrights and actors from across Europe. The 18th century brought about the rise of opera, with venues like the Stadsschouwburg providing a platform for grand productions and performances by renowned composers.

The 19th century marked a significant transformation in the performing arts, with the establishment of new theaters and a shift towards a more commercialized form of entertainment. The advent of melodrama and operetta reflected changing tastes, while the emergence of the bourgeoisie as a dominant social class influenced the themes and styles of performances.

The 20th Century: Innovation and Evolution

The 20th century heralded further innovation in Amsterdam's music and theater scenes. The aftermath of World War II saw a cultural revival, with artists and performers exploring new avenues of expression. The founding of the Netherlands Opera in 1965 and the Concertgebouw Orchestra solidified Amsterdam's reputation as a center for high-quality musical performance. The Concertgebouw, known for its exceptional acoustics, became a premier venue for classical music, attracting world-renowned musicians and conductors.

In parallel, the theater scene expanded to include avant-garde and experimental forms, with the emergence of companies such as the Toneelgroep Amsterdam, which focused on contemporary works and innovative productions. The integration of multimedia and technology into performances began to take shape, reflecting broader societal changes and artistic experimentation.

Contemporary Scene and Global Influence

Today, Amsterdam's music and performing arts scene is characterized by diversity and inclusivity, with genres ranging from classical and jazz to pop and electronic music. Festivals, such as the Amsterdam Dance Event and the Holland Festival, attract international artists and audiences, showcasing the city's role as a global cultural hub.

The city continues to foster new talent through initiatives that support emerging artists, composers, and playwrights. The presence of cultural institutions, such as the Amsterdam University of the Arts, further contributes to the vibrant arts ecosystem.

In conclusion, the development of music and performing arts in Amsterdam is a testament to the city's dynamic history and its ongoing commitment to cultural innovation. From its early roots to its current status as a global cultural capital, Amsterdam's artistic landscape continues to evolve, reflecting the rich interplay of tradition and modernity that defines this unique city.

Museums and Cultural Institutions

Amsterdam, a city known for its rich history and vibrant cultural tapestry, has emerged as a prominent cultural capital over the centuries. A significant aspect of Amsterdam's identity lies in its museums and cultural institutions, which not only preserve but also celebrate the city's artistic heritage and diverse narratives. Among the most notable institutions are the

Rijksmuseum and the Anne Frank House, both of which encapsulate the essence of Amsterdam's cultural evolution.

The Rijksmuseum: A Treasure Trove of Dutch Art

Founded in 1800, the Rijksmuseum is the national museum of the Netherlands and is perhaps the most iconic representation of Amsterdam's cultural legacy. The museum houses an extensive collection of over one million artworks and historical artifacts, with a focus on Dutch art and history. Its most famous pieces include masterpieces by Rembrandt, Vermeer, and Hals, showcasing the pinnacle of the Dutch Golden Age.

The museum underwent a significant renovation, completed in 2013, which transformed it into a modern institution while preserving its historic architecture. This renovation not only enhanced the visitor experience but also reinforced the Rijksmuseum's role as a center for cultural dialogue and education. The museum offers a variety of exhibitions, educational programs, and events that engage diverse audiences, thereby solidifying its status as a cultural beacon in Amsterdam.

The Anne Frank House: A Symbol of Resilience

Another vital institution in Amsterdam is the Anne Frank House, dedicated to the memory of Anne Frank, a Jewish girl who hid from the Nazis during World War II and became a symbol of the human spirit's resilience in the face of oppression. The museum is located in the actual house where Anne and her family sought refuge, and it serves as a powerful reminder of the atrocities of war and the importance of tolerance and human rights.

Since its opening to the public in 1960, the Anne Frank House has attracted millions of visitors from around the globe. The museum not only preserves Anne's diary and personal belongings but also offers educational programs that promote discussions about discrimination, prejudice, and the importance of standing up against injustice. The Anne Frank House plays a crucial role in fostering awareness about the Holocaust and the ongoing relevance of Anne's message, reinforcing Amsterdam's commitment to cultural memory and education.

The Broader Cultural Landscape

Beyond these two institutions, Amsterdam is home to numerous museums and galleries that reflect the city's diverse cultural landscape. The Van Gogh Museum, dedicated to the works of Vincent van Gogh, and the Stedelijk Museum, which focuses on modern and contemporary art, both contribute significantly to the city's cultural offerings. Additionally, smaller galleries and independent art spaces enrich the local scene, showcasing the work of emerging artists and providing a platform for contemporary artistic expression.

Amsterdam's cultural institutions are not static; they actively engage with the community and adapt to contemporary issues. Initiatives such as the "Museum Night" and the "Amsterdam Art Weekend" highlight the city's vibrant art scene and encourage public participation, making culture accessible to all residents and visitors alike.

Conclusion: A Cultural Capital in Flux

In conclusion, Amsterdam's rise as a cultural capital is inextricably linked to its museums and cultural institutions, which serve as custodians of the city's artistic and historical narratives. The Rijksmuseum and the Anne Frank House exemplify this role, offering insights into both the grandeur of Dutch art and the poignant lessons of history. As Amsterdam continues to evolve, its cultural landscape remains a vital part of its identity, fostering dialogue, understanding, and appreciation for the richness of human experience. The city's commitment to preserving its heritage while embracing contemporary narratives ensures that it will remain a beacon of culture for generations to come.

Festivals and Public Celebrations

Amsterdam, a city known for its rich history, vibrant culture, and open-minded ethos, hosts a myriad of festivals and public celebrations throughout the year. These events not only provide entertainment but also serve as a reflection of the city's cultural diversity, historical heritage, and social dynamics. From traditional celebrations that date back centuries to contemporary festivals that embrace modernity, Amsterdam's festivities encapsulate the spirit of its inhabitants and the city's evolution.

One of the most iconic celebrations is King's Day (Koningsdag), held annually on April 27th, marking the birthday of King Willem-Alexander. This national holiday transforms Amsterdam into a sea of orange, as locals and tourists alike don orange attire to show their royal allegiance. The city comes alive with street markets, music, and parties, and the canals are filled with boats hosting celebrations. King's Day exemplifies how a royal celebration fosters a sense of national pride while simultaneously embracing the city's communal spirit.

In contrast, the Amsterdam Pride festival, celebrated in early August, highlights the city's commitment to diversity and inclusion, particularly regarding LGBTQ+ rights. The centerpiece of this event is the renowned Canal Parade, where beautifully decorated boats sail through the waterways, showcasing vibrant performances and messages of love and acceptance. Amsterdam Pride not only celebrates LGBTQ+ culture but also raises awareness for ongoing struggles against discrimination, reflecting the city's progressive values and its historical role as a safe haven for marginalized communities.

Another significant event is the Amsterdam Light Festival, which occurs during the winter months and illuminates the city with stunning light artworks created by international artists. This festival invites visitors to explore the city's canals while experiencing art in a unique, immersive way. By merging creativity with the enchanting winter atmosphere, the festival highlights Amsterdam's cultural vibrancy and its ability to adapt and thrive in different contexts.

The Sinterklaas celebration, leading up to December 5th, showcases Amsterdam's rich traditions and folklore. Sinterklaas, the Dutch version of Santa Claus, arrives by steamboat from Spain, greeted by enthusiastic crowds. The festivities involve parades, gift-giving, and traditional songs, emphasizing the importance of family and community ties. This celebration reveals the unique Dutch customs and highlights how cultural traditions are preserved and celebrated within a modern urban environment.

Additionally, the Holland Festival, held every June, is a platform for international performing arts, showcasing theater, dance, opera, and music. This festival emphasizes Amsterdam's role as a cultural capital, drawing talent from all over the world and celebrating artistic expression. By presenting diverse artistic forms, the Holland Festival underscores the city's commitment to fostering a rich cultural dialogue and its historical position as a melting pot of ideas and influences.

Moreover, Amsterdam's Street Markets and local celebrations like Oud & Nieuw (New Year's Eve) and Nationale Molendag (National Windmill Day) reflect grassroots involvement and the communal aspect of the city's culture. These events encourage local participation and promote the unique character of Amsterdam's neighborhoods, further enriching the city's cultural tapestry.

In conclusion, festivals and public celebrations in Amsterdam serve as a vibrant expression of the city's cultural diversity and historical richness. They not only entertain but also educate, foster community ties, and promote social values, reflecting the dynamic and inclusive nature of Amsterdam's society. Through these celebrations, residents and visitors alike engage with the city's heritage and embrace its continually evolving identity, ensuring that Amsterdam remains a vibrant cultural hub on the global stage.

Chapter 13

Amsterdam's Role in Dutch Politics

The Formation of the Dutch Republic

The establishment of the Dutch Republic in the late 16th century marked a pivotal moment in European history, characterized by the assertion of independence from Spanish rule and the emergence of a unique political entity that would become a beacon of trade, culture, and republican governance. Central to this transformative period was Amsterdam, which not only served as a key economic hub but also played an instrumental role in the political developments that shaped the nascent Republic.

As discontent simmered in the northern provinces of the Low Countries, primarily due to oppressive taxation and religious persecution under the rule of Philip II of Spain, the desire for autonomy grew stronger. The Eighty Years' War (1568–1648) was a protracted conflict that epitomized this struggle, and it was in this context that Amsterdam's significance began to rise. With its thriving economy bolstered by maritime trade and a burgeoning merchant class, Amsterdam provided both the financial resources and political impetus necessary for the rebellion against Spanish authority.

The city's strategic location along trade routes made it a vital port, facilitating commerce and the influx of wealth. This economic power translated into political influence, as the city became a hub for revolutionary ideas and the organization of resistance against Spanish rule. The "Watergeuzen", a group of Dutch sea rebels, famously seized Brielle in 1572, marking a significant turning point in the revolt. This victory not only galvanized support for the rebellion but also highlighted Amsterdam's role as a center of revolutionary action.

In 1579, the Union of Utrecht was signed, a crucial agreement among the northern provinces that laid the groundwork for the formation of the Dutch Republic. Amsterdam was a key player in this union, persuading other provinces to join the cause and adopting a stance that emphasized collective defense and mutual support against Spanish aggression. The Union effectively articulated the desire for independence, asserting the sovereignty of the provinces and setting the stage for the formal establishment of the Republic in 1588.

As the Dutch Republic took shape, Amsterdam emerged as its de facto capital. The political structure of the Republic was unique, characterized by a decentralized governance model that allowed for significant autonomy among its constituent cities. However, Amsterdam wielded considerable influence within this framework, primarily due to its economic clout and the prominence of its civic leaders, known as the "regents." These patrician families dominated the political landscape, steering the Republic's policies and engaging in diplomacy that would enhance its international standing.

The Amsterdam City Council became a powerful institution, playing a crucial role in governance and the formulation of policies that guided the Republic's development. The city's leaders were adept at navigating the complexities of both local and international politics, forging alliances that benefited Amsterdam's interests. They played a key role in the administration of trade policies, naval expansion, and the establishment of the Dutch East India Company (VOC), which would become a linchpin of the Republic's economic might.

Moreover, Amsterdam's cultural and intellectual environment flourished during this period, fostering a spirit of innovation and inquiry that contributed to the Republic's identity. The interplay between commerce, governance, and culture established Amsterdam as a model of republicanism, influencing other cities and regions.

In conclusion, Amsterdam's role in the formation and governance of the Dutch Republic was multifaceted, encompassing economic power, political leadership, and cultural vitality. The city's emergence as a center of resistance against Spanish rule and its subsequent influence in the Republic's governance laid the foundations for a society that valued trade, tolerance, and civic engagement, leaving a lasting legacy that would resonate throughout European history.

Amsterdam and the Dutch Monarchy

Amsterdam has played a pivotal role in shaping the Dutch monarchy, both through its historical significance as the country's economic powerhouse and its cultural influence. The city's interactions with the royal family reflect a complex relationship that has evolved over centuries, marked by periods of collaboration, tension, and mutual dependence.

Historical Context

The roots of Amsterdam's connection to the Dutch monarchy can be traced back to the establishment of the Dutch Republic in the late 16th century. During this time, Amsterdam emerged as a commercial hub, gaining immense wealth and political power. The city's prosperity allowed it to assert significant influence over national affairs, including the monarchy. The House of Orange-Nassau, which produced the monarchs of the Netherlands, found in Amsterdam a vital ally. The city's merchants and political leaders supported the royal family financially and politically, especially during times of conflict, such as the Eighty Years' War against Spanish rule.

In the 17th century, as the Dutch Republic reached its zenith, the relationship between Amsterdam and the monarchy solidified. The city became a center for the arts, sciences, and trade, with the royal family often participating in the cultural and economic life of Amsterdam. This partnership was exemplified by the patronage of artists like Rembrandt and Vermeer, who were commissioned by wealthy Amsterdam merchants and, by extension, the monarchy.

The Monarchy During the Napoleonic Era
The Napoleonic Wars in the early 19th century marked a turning point in this relationship. The French occupation of the Netherlands led to the abolition of the Dutch Republic and the establishment of the Kingdom of Holland under Louis Bonaparte, Napoleon's brother. The upheaval caused by these events resulted in a temporary weakening of Amsterdam's influence, but it also paved the way for the restoration of the monarchy in the form of King William I in 1815. Under his reign, Amsterdam was reaffirmed as a key city in the new Kingdom of the Netherlands, and the royal family began to take a more active role in the city's affairs.

The 20th Century and Royal Ceremonies
Throughout the 20th century, Amsterdam has continued to serve as a backdrop for significant royal events. The city has hosted numerous royal ceremonies, including coronations, anniversaries, and state visits. The most notable of these was the celebration of Queen Beatrix's accession to the throne in 1980, which saw extensive festivities throughout the city. Such events not only underscored the monarchy's connection to Amsterdam but also showcased the city's cultural vitality and historical grandeur.

The royal family has also taken a keen interest in various social issues affecting Amsterdam, such as urban development and cultural heritage. Members of the royal family frequently engage with local communities and support initiatives aimed at preserving the city's rich architectural history and promoting social cohesion.

Contemporary Relations
In recent years, the relationship between Amsterdam and the Dutch monarchy has evolved alongside the city's changing dynamics. The royal family has embraced modern values of inclusivity and sustainability, aligning with Amsterdam's identity as a progressive city. King Willem-Alexander and Queen Maxima have participated in various initiatives promoting social

welfare and cultural diversity, reflecting their commitment to the well-being of all citizens, including those in Amsterdam.

Moreover, Amsterdam's reputation as an international city has drawn the royal family into global dialogues, particularly regarding issues like climate change and social justice. This engagement demonstrates how the monarchy continues to adapt to contemporary challenges while maintaining its historical ties to the city.

Conclusion

In summary, the relationship between Amsterdam and the Dutch monarchy is characterized by mutual influence and historical significance. From the early days of the Dutch Republic to the present, this dynamic has shaped both the city and the royal family. As Amsterdam continues to evolve in the 21st century, the monarchy remains an integral part of its identity, bridging historical traditions with modern values and aspirations.

The Influence of Amsterdam on National Policy

Amsterdam, as the capital and largest city of the Netherlands, has played a pivotal role in shaping the country's social, economic, and foreign policies throughout its history. The city's strategic location, rich cultural heritage, and historical significance have made it a central hub for political discourse and policy-making, particularly during critical periods such as the establishment of the Dutch Republic, the Golden Age, and beyond.

Economic Policies

During the 17th century, Amsterdam emerged as one of the world's leading financial centers, a development that had profound implications for national economic policy. The establishment of the Amsterdam Stock Exchange in 1602 marked the beginning of modern financial markets, allowing for unprecedented capital mobilization. This financial innovation enabled the Dutch East India Company (VOC) to thrive, influencing national policies that favored trade expansion and colonial endeavors. The wealth generated by trade not only enriched the city but also provided the Dutch government with the resources necessary to pursue military campaigns and engage in international diplomacy.

Furthermore, as the hub of Dutch commerce, Amsterdam's policies on trade, including tariffs and trade agreements, influenced national economic strategies. The city's merchants and traders were crucial in shaping the Republic's mercantilist policies, advocating for free trade and open markets, which became a cornerstone of Dutch economic ideology. This foundation allowed the Netherlands to become a global trading power, setting precedents in economic policy that would resonate for centuries.

Social Policies

Amsterdam has also been a significant influence on social policies within the Netherlands. The city's diverse population, historically a melting pot of various cultures, ideologies, and religions, has prompted progressive social reforms. During the late 19th and early 20th centuries, Amsterdam became a center for labor movements and social activism. The rise of socialist and labor parties in the city influenced national discussions on workers' rights, leading to reforms such as improved labor laws and social welfare programs.

Moreover, Amsterdam's experience with immigration and multiculturalism has shaped national policies on integration and social cohesion. The city has often served as a testing ground for progressive social initiatives aimed at promoting equality and diversity, influencing the wider Dutch approach to social justice and community relations. The debates surrounding these issues in Amsterdam have frequently reached the national level, prompting policymakers to consider more inclusive practices that reflect the city's realities.

Foreign Policies

In terms of foreign policy, Amsterdam has historically been at the forefront of Dutch diplomatic relations. The city was instrumental in establishing the Netherlands as a sovereign state following the Eighty Years' War, and it continues to host numerous international organizations and embassies, reinforcing its role as a diplomatic hub. The city's international orientation has shaped national policies regarding European integration, international trade agreements, and global cooperation in areas such as climate change.

Moreover, Amsterdam's historical engagement in global trade has influenced the Netherlands' foreign policy priorities, particularly in fostering strong economic ties with emerging markets. The city's proactive approach to international relations exemplifies the Dutch commitment to multilateralism, often advocating for collaborative solutions to global challenges.

Conclusion

In conclusion, Amsterdam's influence on national policy in the Netherlands is profound and multifaceted, encompassing economic, social, and foreign policy dimensions. As a dynamic city with a rich history of trade and diversity, Amsterdam has not only shaped the policies that govern its own populace but has also had a lasting impact on the broader national landscape. The lessons learned from Amsterdam's historical experiences continue to inform contemporary debates, ensuring that the city remains a vital contributor to the Netherlands' ongoing evolution in policy-making and governance.

Amsterdam as a Capital City

Amsterdam, often referred to as the cultural heart of the Netherlands, serves a dual role as both the economic and cultural capital of the nation. This balancing act is deeply rooted in the city's historical evolution, geographical advantages, and its ongoing commitment to innovation and inclusivity.

Historically, Amsterdam's prominence as a trading hub dates back to the 17th century, during the Dutch Golden Age, when it emerged as one of the world's leading centers for commerce and finance. The establishment of the Dutch East India Company (VOC) not only bolstered the city's economic framework but also laid the foundation for a diverse and prosperous society. This economic vitality attracted people from various backgrounds, fostering a multicultural environment that has become a hallmark of Amsterdam today. The city's role as the financial epicenter of the Netherlands is exemplified by institutions such as the Amsterdam Stock Exchange, which is widely considered the oldest stock exchange in the world.

In recent years, Amsterdam has transformed into a modern economic powerhouse, with a focus on technology, innovation, and sustainability. The city's strategic location as a gateway to Europe, coupled with its advanced infrastructure, has made it a favorable destination for international businesses. The presence of multinational companies and start-ups has further solidified Amsterdam's status as an economic capital, contributing significantly to its GDP and job creation. The city also hosts various international conferences and trade fairs, showcasing its pivotal role in global commerce.

Culturally, Amsterdam is equally significant. As a UNESCO World Heritage site, the city boasts an array of world-class museums, galleries, and theaters. Institutions such as the Rijksmuseum, the Van Gogh Museum, and the Anne Frank House not only attract millions of visitors each year but also play a vital role in preserving and promoting Dutch heritage. The city's commitment to the arts is evident in its vibrant cultural scene, which includes theater productions, music festivals, and public art installations. This cultural richness enhances Amsterdam's identity as a cosmopolitan city, where art and history intermingle with modernity.

The balance between Amsterdam's roles as an economic and cultural capital is evident in its urban planning and policy-making. The city's administration actively promotes initiatives that integrate economic development with cultural enrichment. For instance, urban renewal projects often include provisions for cultural spaces, ensuring that as the city grows economically, its cultural fabric remains intact and vibrant. Furthermore, the city invests in public spaces, parks, and community centers that encourage social interaction and cultural exchange, fostering a sense of belonging among residents.

However, this balance is not without challenges. The rapid growth of the housing market, driven by an influx of residents and international companies, has led to rising living costs and concerns about gentrification. The city's administration is actively addressing these issues through policies aimed at increasing affordable housing, preserving cultural sites, and ensuring that the benefits of economic growth are distributed equitably among its inhabitants.

In conclusion, Amsterdam's dual identity as both the economic and cultural capital of the Netherlands is a dynamic interplay that shapes the city's identity. Its historical legacy as a trading hub, combined with a commitment to cultural preservation and social inclusivity, allows Amsterdam to thrive in a globalized world. As the city continues to evolve, its ability to balance these roles will be crucial in maintaining its status as a leading city on both national and international stages, ensuring that it remains a vibrant, diverse, and prosperous metropolis for generations to come.

Major Political Movements in Amsterdam

Amsterdam has long been recognized as a pivotal center of political activism and reform, reflecting broader societal changes in the Netherlands and influencing global political thought. This legacy is deeply rooted in the city's history, where diverse social movements have emerged, driven by the quest for equality, justice, and democratic participation.

The Rise of Republicanism

The political landscape of Amsterdam began to take shape in the late 16th and early 17th centuries, during the Dutch Revolt against Spanish rule. The city became a bastion of republicanism, advocating for self-governance and opposing monarchical tyranny. The establishment of the Dutch Republic in 1581 marked a significant turning point; Amsterdam's merchants and civic leaders played a crucial role in promoting the ideas of democracy and civic freedom, contributing to the formulation of a political system that favored a decentralized governance structure.

The Age of Enlightenment

In the 18th century, Amsterdam emerged as a hub for Enlightenment thought. The city became home to influential philosophers such as Baruch Spinoza and later, the radical thinker Hermanus Boerhaave, who championed reason, science, and secularism. The ideas propagated during this era laid the groundwork for subsequent political movements, emphasizing individual rights and challenging the status quo. The Enlightenment's ideals resonated with citizens, leading to calls for reform in governance and social structure.

The Labor Movement

The industrialization of the 19th century brought significant social and economic upheaval, resulting in the rise of the labor movement. Workers in Amsterdam began organizing to demand better working conditions, fair wages, and the right to collective bargaining. The establishment of labor unions during this period galvanized the working class, leading to strikes and protests that highlighted the struggles of urban workers. Political parties, particularly the

Social Democratic Workers' Party (SDAP), emerged to represent these interests, significantly shaping the political discourse of the era.

Women's Suffrage and Feminism
The early 20th century witnessed the rise of the women's suffrage movement, with Amsterdam at the forefront. Activists like Aletta Jacobs campaigned tirelessly for women's rights, including the right to vote, access to education, and reproductive rights. The movement gained momentum during and after World War I, culminating in women gaining the right to vote in 1919. Amsterdam became a hotbed for feminist thought, influencing broader societal changes regarding gender equality.

Anti-War and Peace Movements
The interwar period saw the emergence of various anti-war movements in Amsterdam, spurred by the devastating impacts of World War I and the rise of militarism in Europe. Activists organized rallies, advocated for disarmament, and promoted pacifism, contributing to a culture of peace that persisted through the tumultuous years of World War II. The horrors of the Nazi occupation galvanized further political activism, with many citizens participating in resistance efforts against the occupiers.

Environmental and Social Justice Movements
In the latter half of the 20th century, Amsterdam became a focal point for environmental activism and social justice movements. The 1960s and 70s saw the rise of the Provo movement, which challenged conventional social norms and advocated for a more inclusive, just society. Subsequently, movements addressing issues such as housing rights, racial equality, and LGBTQ+ rights gained traction, reflecting the city's commitment to progressive values.

Contemporary Activism
Today, Amsterdam remains a vibrant center for political activism, with ongoing movements addressing climate change, immigration policies, and social equality. The city's diverse population continues to advocate for justice and reform, ensuring that Amsterdam's legacy as a center of political thought and action endures.

In conclusion, Amsterdam's history of political activism is characterized by a rich tapestry of movements, each contributing to the city's identity as a progressive hub for reform and social change. The political struggles and successes of its citizens have not only shaped local governance but have also resonated across national and international landscapes, making Amsterdam a vital player in the quest for justice, equality, and human rights.

Chapter 14

Amsterdam in International Relations

Amsterdam's Role in the European Union

Amsterdam, the capital of the Netherlands, has played a significant role in the evolution of the European Union (EU), not just as a political entity but as a cultural and economic hub that has shaped international relations within Europe and beyond. The city's strategic geographic location, coupled with its rich history of trade and diplomacy, has established it as a critical player in EU affairs.

One of the most notable aspects of Amsterdam's role within the EU is its historical significance in the formation of European governance structures. The Treaty of Amsterdam, signed in 1997, marked a pivotal moment in EU history, enhancing the powers of the European Parliament and setting the stage for further integration among member states. This treaty, named after the city, symbolizes Amsterdam's stature as a center for European diplomacy and decision-making. It reflects the city's long-standing tradition of fostering dialogue and consensus among diverse nations, a trait deeply rooted in its mercantile past.

Amsterdam's influence extends beyond treaties; it serves as the host city for several important EU agencies and institutions. The European headquarters of various organizations, including the European Monitoring Centre for Drugs and Drug Addiction (EMCDDA) and the European Institute for Gender Equality (EIGE), are located in the city. These institutions play crucial roles in shaping EU policies on health, gender equality, and social issues. The presence of these agencies not only amplifies Amsterdam's voice in EU policymaking but also attracts professionals and experts from across Europe, enhancing the city's reputation as a center for international cooperation and governance.

Moreover, Amsterdam's vibrant economy, heavily reliant on international trade and finance, positions it as a key economic player within the EU. The city's port, one of the largest in Europe, serves as a vital gateway for goods entering and leaving the continent. This economic dynamism has enabled Amsterdam to contribute significantly to the EU's internal market, promoting trade liberalization and economic cooperation among member states. The city's financial institutions, including the Amsterdam Stock Exchange, one of the oldest in the world, facilitate investment and capital flows, further integrating the Netherlands within the EU economy.

Culturally, Amsterdam embodies the European ideal of diversity and inclusion. The city is home to a rich tapestry of cultures, a testament to the EU's foundational principle of promoting unity within diversity. This multicultural environment fosters innovation and creativity, making Amsterdam a fertile ground for cultural exchange and collaboration. The city's hosting of various international festivals, conferences, and cultural events enhances its profile as a cosmopolitan center, reinforcing the EU's objectives of cooperation and understanding among its member states.

However, Amsterdam's role within the EU is not without challenges. As the EU faces pressing issues such as migration, climate change, and economic inequality, Amsterdam must navigate complex international relations while advocating for policies that reflect its values of social justice and sustainability. The city's active participation in EU discussions on these topics underscores its commitment to shaping a more equitable and environmentally conscious Europe.

In conclusion, Amsterdam's position within the European Union is multifaceted, encompassing historical, political, economic, and cultural dimensions. The city has not only contributed to the development of EU policies and institutions but has also leveraged its unique attributes to enhance its international relations. As the EU continues to evolve, Amsterdam remains a vital player, committed to fostering cooperation and addressing the challenges of a rapidly changing world. The city's legacy of trade, diplomacy, and cultural richness will undoubtedly influence its future role in the European Union and the broader global landscape.

Amsterdam and Global Trade

Amsterdam's evolution into a global trade hub began in the late Middle Ages, with its strategic location along the Amstel River facilitating access to both inland and maritime routes. The city's early development as a trading post was significantly bolstered by its incorporation into the Hanseatic League, a powerful alliance of merchant guilds and market towns in Northwestern Europe. Although Amsterdam was not an official member, it benefited from the trade networks established by the League, allowing it to engage in the lucrative trade of goods such as herring, textiles, and grain.

By the 17th century, often referred to as the Dutch Golden Age, Amsterdam ascended to unparalleled heights in global trade, largely due to the establishment of the Dutch East India Company (VOC) in 1602. This was one of the world's first multinational corporations, and it played a vital role in expanding Amsterdam's influence across Asia and beyond. The VOC monopolized the spice trade, importing valuable commodities such as nutmeg, cloves, and pepper from the East Indies and establishing a network of trading posts and colonies. The immense wealth generated by the VOC led to the construction of the iconic canal ring that characterizes Amsterdam's landscape today, as merchants reinvested their profits into the city's infrastructure.

Amsterdam's role as a financial center further solidified its status in global trade. The city became the birthplace of modern banking practices, with the establishment of the Amsterdam Stock Exchange in 1602, which facilitated the trading of shares and bonds. This not only provided capital for trade expeditions but also attracted investors from across Europe, cementing Amsterdam's reputation as a financial hub. The city's innovative financial instruments, including bills of exchange and insurance, facilitated international trade transactions and reduced the risks associated with long-distance shipping.

As the 18th century approached, Amsterdam faced challenges such as wars and the decline of the VOC due to increased competition from rival powers. However, the city adapted by diversifying its economy and trade networks. In the 19th century, during the Industrial Revolution, Amsterdam transitioned from a trade-based economy to one that embraced industrialization and manufacturing. The city leveraged its historical trading expertise to become a pivotal player in European trade networks, focusing on industries such as shipbuilding, textiles, and later, machinery.

In the contemporary context, Amsterdam remains a vital node in global trade, but the nature of its role has evolved. The city has embraced globalization, positioning itself as a center for trade, logistics, and technology. The Port of Amsterdam, one of the largest ports in Europe, plays a crucial role in the import and export of goods, supporting a wide range of industries from food to chemicals. Amsterdam's connectivity is enhanced by its extensive transport infrastructure, including Schiphol Airport, which facilitates international trade and travel.

Moreover, Amsterdam has adapted to the challenges of the 21st century by focusing on sustainable trade practices and innovation. The city is increasingly emphasizing its commitment to sustainability, aiming to become a leader in sustainable logistics and green trade initiatives. This includes investments in renewable energy, sustainable transport solutions, and policies aimed at reducing carbon emissions in trade-related activities.

In summary, Amsterdam's historical and contemporary role in global trade networks is characterized by its adaptability and resilience. From its origins as a fishing village to its rise as a financial powerhouse and global trade center, the city continues to navigate the complexities of international commerce while embracing sustainable practices that will shape its future in an interconnected world.

Diplomatic Presence in Amsterdam

Amsterdam, the capital of the Netherlands, has long been recognized not only for its rich cultural heritage and economic vitality but also for its significant role in international diplomacy. The city hosts a variety of diplomatic missions, including embassies, consulates, and international organizations, which collectively reinforce its status as a vital hub for global diplomacy and cooperation.

Embassies and Consulates

Although The Hague is the seat of the Dutch government and home to the majority of foreign embassies in the Netherlands, Amsterdam plays a complementary role by hosting several important consulates and honorary consulates. These diplomatic missions serve as vital points of contact for foreign nationals and businesses, facilitating trade and investment relationships. The presence of these consulates enhances the city's global connectivity, allowing international visitors and expatriates to access their home country's services easily.

Consulates in Amsterdam cater to a diverse range of countries, reflecting the city's multicultural population. They engage in various activities, from issuing visas and providing assistance to nationals in distress, to promoting bilateral trade and cultural exchanges. This multifaceted role underscores the importance of Amsterdam as a gateway for international relations, wherein local officials and diplomats work collaboratively to strengthen diplomatic ties.

International Organizations

In addition to diplomatic missions, Amsterdam is home to numerous international organizations that contribute to its diplomatic significance. The city has been a center for various non-governmental organizations (NGOs), international institutions, and think tanks. These organizations address a plethora of global issues, including human rights, environmental sustainability, and economic development. The presence of these entities not only shapes Amsterdam's international profile but also stimulates local discussions on global challenges.

One notable organization is the International Court of Justice (ICJ), located in The Hague, which occasionally collaborates with Amsterdam-based institutions for conferences and discussions that influence international law and diplomacy. Furthermore, Amsterdam is also the headquarters for several EU agencies and organizations that focus on areas such as public health and safety, enhancing the city's role in European and global governance.

Cultural Diplomacy

Cultural diplomacy is another significant aspect of Amsterdam's diplomatic presence. The city is known for its vibrant arts scene, which plays a crucial role in fostering cultural exchanges between nations. Events such as the Amsterdam Dance Event and the International Documentary Film Festival attract international participants, providing a platform for dialogue and collaboration among artists, policymakers, and cultural institutions.

Additionally, Amsterdam's rich history of tolerance and diversity has positioned it as a city that promotes intercultural dialogue. This ethos is reflected in various cultural programs and initiatives that encourage international cooperation and understanding, further solidifying its status as a diplomatic center.

Conclusion

The diplomatic presence in Amsterdam, characterized by its consulates, international organizations, and cultural initiatives, significantly enhances the city's stature on the global stage. By serving as a nexus for international diplomacy, Amsterdam not only facilitates dialogue and cooperation among nations but also promotes its own interests in trade, culture, and political discourse. As global challenges continue to evolve, the role of Amsterdam in international relations will likely expand, ensuring that the city remains a crucial player in shaping the future of diplomacy and global governance.

The Impact of International Organizations on Amsterdam's Global Standing

Amsterdam has long been a city of global significance, not only due to its rich history of trade and cultural exchange but also because of its strategic role as a hub for international organizations. Over the years, institutions like the International Criminal Court (ICC) and the United Nations (UN) have established their presence in the city, further elevating Amsterdam's position on the global stage. This involvement has enhanced the city's reputation as a center for diplomacy, international law, and humanitarian efforts.

The establishment of the ICC in The Hague, located just a short distance from Amsterdam, marked a significant milestone in international law and justice. Founded in 2002, the ICC is responsible for prosecuting individuals for genocide, war crimes, and crimes against humanity. Its proximity to Amsterdam has facilitated the city's role as an essential hub for legal experts, diplomats, and international activists dedicated to the promotion of human rights and the rule of law. This presence has attracted a diverse community of professionals and institutions, fostering a culture of legal scholarship and advocacy that has benefitted both the city and the broader international community.

Moreover, Amsterdam's status as a host city for various UN agencies, including the United Nations Office on Drugs and Crime (UNODC) and the United Nations International Strategy for Disaster Reduction (UNISDR), has underscored its commitment to addressing pressing global issues. These organizations focus on critical matters such as drug control, crime prevention, and disaster risk reduction, which are increasingly relevant in today's interconnected world. The presence of these agencies has not only allowed Amsterdam to contribute to global policymaking but has also positioned the city as a center for research, innovation, and capacity-building in these important areas.

In addition to hosting international organizations, Amsterdam has become a popular venue for conferences, summits, and forums that address global challenges such as climate change, sustainable development, and social justice. Events such as the Amsterdam International Water Week and the annual Amsterdam Conference on the Human Rights of Migrants attract participants from around the world, facilitating dialogue and collaboration among governments, NGOs, and civil society. This active engagement in global discussions helps to reinforce Amsterdam's image as a city committed to finding solutions to international problems.

Furthermore, the city's multi-faceted role in international relations is complemented by its cultural and educational institutions, which provide a rich backdrop for discussions on global governance. The presence of universities and research organizations dedicated to international relations, law, and social sciences enhances the city's intellectual capacity, drawing scholars and practitioners alike who seek to engage with pressing global issues.

Amsterdam's global standing is also strengthened by its commitment to sustainability and social equity, principles that resonate with many international organizations. As the city grapples with challenges such as climate change, urbanization, and social inequality, its strategies and policies can serve as models for other cities worldwide. By aligning its local initiatives with the goals of international organizations, Amsterdam not only addresses its own challenges but also contributes to global efforts aimed at creating a more sustainable and equitable world.

In conclusion, the impact of international organizations like the ICC and the UN on Amsterdam's global standing is profound and multifaceted. Their presence has solidified the city's role as a center for diplomacy and international cooperation while fostering a vibrant community dedicated to addressing global challenges. As Amsterdam continues to navigate the complexities of an increasingly interconnected world, its ongoing engagement with international organizations will undoubtedly shape its future trajectory and enhance its influence on the global stage.

Amsterdam's Role in Global Environmental Initiatives

Amsterdam has long been at the forefront of sustainability and environmental consciousness, establishing itself as a model for urban environmental initiatives that address climate change and promote sustainable living. This commitment is reflected in a multifaceted approach that combines innovative policies, community engagement, and international collaboration.

One of the most significant aspects of Amsterdam's environmental agenda is its ambitious climate policy, which aims to reduce greenhouse gas emissions by 55% by 2030 compared to 1990 levels. The city's Climate Action Plan outlines comprehensive strategies for achieving this goal, including the promotion of renewable energy, energy efficiency in buildings, and the electrification of transportation. Amsterdam has invested heavily in solar energy, with thousands of solar panels installed across rooftops, further enhancing its renewable energy portfolio.

Transportation is another critical area where Amsterdam has made significant strides in sustainability. The city is renowned for its extensive cycling infrastructure, which encourages residents to opt for bicycles over cars. The city boasts over 500 kilometers of dedicated bike lanes, making cycling not only a favored mode of transport but also an integral part of Amsterdam's culture. In addition to cycling, the city has promoted electric vehicles (EVs) by expanding charging infrastructure and incentivizing EV ownership through subsidies and reduced parking fees. As a result, Amsterdam aims to have all public transport operated by zero-emission vehicles by 2025, further decreasing its carbon footprint.

Moreover, Amsterdam's commitment to sustainability extends to its urban planning and public spaces. The city has adopted the concept of the "circular economy," which emphasizes reducing waste and reusing materials. Initiatives such as the Amsterdam Circular Strategy aim to make the city fully circular by 2050, focusing on waste reduction, resource efficiency, and the sustainable use of materials. This approach includes promoting local businesses that adhere to circular principles and encouraging citizens to participate in recycling and waste reduction programs.

Amsterdam's role in global environmental initiatives is further solidified through its participation in international organizations and forums. The city has been a key player in the C40 Cities Climate Leadership Group, a network of the world's megacities committed to addressing climate change and driving urban action that reduces greenhouse gas emissions. Through this platform, Amsterdam shares best practices and collaborates with other cities to implement effective climate solutions.

Additionally, Amsterdam hosts the Amsterdam International WaterWeek, a biennial event that brings together global experts to discuss water management and sustainability challenges. This conference highlights Amsterdam's leadership in water technology and its innovative approaches to tackling issues such as flooding, water quality, and resource management—all crucial in the context of climate change.

Community engagement is also vital to Amsterdam's environmental strategy. The city actively involves its residents in sustainability initiatives through campaigns aimed at raising awareness about climate change and encouraging eco-friendly practices. Programs like "Green Amsterdam" facilitate community-led projects that promote urban greening, biodiversity, and sustainable living, ensuring that citizens are not just passive recipients of policy but active participants in shaping a sustainable future.

In conclusion, Amsterdam's role in global environmental initiatives is characterized by proactive policies, innovative urban planning, community engagement, and international cooperation. The city exemplifies how urban centers can lead the charge in sustainability, serving as a blueprint for others worldwide. As climate change continues to pose significant threats, Amsterdam's efforts underscore the critical importance of integrated, city-wide strategies to foster resilience and sustainability in the face of global challenges.

Chapter 15

Conclusion and Reflections

Summary of Amsterdam's Historical Development

Amsterdam's history is a rich tapestry woven through centuries of transformation, marked by pivotal events and key periods that have shaped its identity. The city's origins trace back to the late 12th century, when small fishing settlements emerged along the banks of the Amstel River. These early communities laid the groundwork for what would become a bustling urban center. The construction of the dam in the Amstel around which the city was named not only facilitated local trade but also catalyzed Amsterdam's growth into a significant commercial hub.

By the early 14th century, Amsterdam had gained its first city charter in 1300, solidifying its status and governance. This period heralded the growth of trade routes and commerce, which became the lifeblood of the city. The burgeoning trade networks, particularly with the Hanseatic League, allowed Amsterdam to flourish economically, attracting merchants and establishing the foundations of a diverse marketplace.

The 17th century marked the Golden Age of Amsterdam, a time characterized by the rise of the Dutch East India Company (VOC). This period not only brought immense wealth to the city but also positioned Amsterdam as a global trading powerhouse. It became a financial center, leading the world in banking and stock trading. The flourishing arts scene produced masterpieces from renowned figures like Rembrandt and Vermeer, while the city's architectural landscape transformed with the construction of its iconic canals and merchant houses.

However, the 18th century ushered in challenges, as the decline of Dutch power, exacerbated by wars and economic downturns, diminished Amsterdam's prominence. The French occupation under Napoleon further complicated the city's trajectory, leading to significant social and economic changes. Despite these adversities, the Enlightenment brought a wave of intellectual vigor that reshaped Amsterdam's political and cultural landscape.

The 19th century heralded the Kingdom of the Netherlands, which saw Amsterdam evolve amid industrialization and urbanization. This period was marked by rising factories, changing labor dynamics, and the emergence of social reform movements advocating for workers' rights and better living conditions. Amidst rapid growth, Amsterdam faced housing crises, prompting urban development initiatives that addressed the needs of its burgeoning population.

The impact of World War I was felt keenly in Amsterdam, as the city navigated its neutral status, grappling with economic challenges while maintaining social stability. The post-war recovery fostered modernization, setting the stage for the dynamic changes of the interwar period.

World War II brought devastation, particularly upon Amsterdam's Jewish community during the Holocaust. The Nazi occupation left deep scars on the city, but post-war reconstruction efforts, supported by international aid through the Marshall Plan, revitalized Amsterdam's economy and infrastructure.

The second half of the 20th century was a period of significant social change, characterized by countercultural movements in the 1960s and 1970s, the rise of the welfare state, and increasing diversity through immigration. The city embraced economic liberalization in the 1980s and 1990s, shifting towards a service-based economy and grappling with the challenges of multiculturalism.

Entering the new millennium, Amsterdam emerged as a globalized city, facing the complexities of sustainability, technological innovation, and social inclusion. With ongoing urban planning efforts, Amsterdam strives to balance its rich historical legacy with contemporary demands, continuing to be a vibrant hub of culture, economics, and international relations.

In summary, Amsterdam's historical development reflects a city that has continuously adapted to challenges and opportunities across the centuries. From its humble beginnings as a fishing village to its current status as a global city, the enduring legacy of Amsterdam is one of resilience, innovation, and cultural richness, setting a compelling example for cities worldwide.

The Enduring Legacy of Amsterdam

Amsterdam, a city steeped in a rich tapestry of history, has evolved over the centuries into a vibrant metropolis that reflects the complexities of its past. The enduring legacy of Amsterdam is evident in various aspects of contemporary life, from its innovative urban planning and commitment to sustainability to its cultural vibrancy and social policies. Each era of the city's history has contributed layers to its identity, shaping how Amsterdam interacts with the world today.

One of the most significant legacies is Amsterdam's historical role as a trading hub. Established during the late Middle Ages, the city's strategic location along the Amstel River allowed it to flourish as a center of commerce. The Dutch East India Company (VOC), which emerged during the 17th century, not only propelled Amsterdam to global prominence but also laid the groundwork for modern capitalism. Today, Amsterdam continues to be a vital player in international trade and finance, with its port serving as a key entry point for goods entering Europe. The city's financial district, including institutions like the Amsterdam Stock Exchange, retains its reputation as one of the leading financial centers, influencing global economic trends.

Moreover, Amsterdam's architectural and urban design heritage profoundly impacts its present-day environment. The iconic canal system, a UNESCO World Heritage site, is not just a historical remnant but an active component of the city's identity and infrastructure. The principles of harmonious urban planning that characterized the Golden Age are revisited in modern development projects. Today, there is a concerted effort to integrate green spaces and sustainable practices into urban planning, reflecting a forward-thinking approach that honors historical aesthetics while addressing contemporary ecological challenges.

Culturally, Amsterdam's legacy is palpable in its thriving arts scene. The contributions of Dutch masters such as Rembrandt and Vermeer continue to resonate, drawing millions of visitors to museums like the Rijksmuseum and the Van Gogh Museum each year. This rich cultural heritage fosters a sense of pride and identity among residents while attracting a global audience, emphasizing Amsterdam's role as a cultural capital. Furthermore, the city's historical commitment to tolerance and diversity informs its current social policies, promoting inclusivity and multiculturalism. This ethos has made Amsterdam a haven for artists, thinkers, and innovators from around the world.

Socially, the legacy of Amsterdam's historical movements—such as the fight for civil rights and labor reforms—shapes the city's contemporary social fabric. The welfare state, which emerged from the social reform movements of the 19th and 20th centuries, has evolved into a robust system supporting social equity and public welfare. Current debates surrounding social justice, housing affordability, and immigration policy are deeply rooted in the historical struggles and triumphs of the city's inhabitants. Thus, the lessons learned from Amsterdam's history guide ongoing discussions about social responsibility and community well-being.

In terms of international influence, Amsterdam's legacy as a center of diplomacy and global cooperation continues to thrive. The city hosts numerous international organizations, including the International Criminal Court and various NGOs focused on humanitarian issues, environmental sustainability, and global governance. This historical engagement in global affairs positions Amsterdam as a proactive player in addressing contemporary challenges, from climate change to human rights.

In conclusion, the enduring legacy of Amsterdam is woven into the very fabric of the city—its economy, culture, social policies, and international standing. The lessons of Amsterdam's past not only shape its present identity but also illuminate pathways for future development. As the city navigates the complexities of globalization and urbanization, its rich history remains a guiding force, ensuring that the spirit of innovation, tolerance, and resilience continues to thrive in the heart of Amsterdam.

Lessons from Amsterdam's History

Amsterdam's rich historical tapestry offers valuable lessons for cities and societies grappling with modern challenges. From its early days as a small settlement to its rise as a global financial hub, Amsterdam exemplifies resilience, adaptability, and innovation. Here are several key takeaways from Amsterdam's journey that can serve as a guide for other urban centers.

1. Embrace Diversity and Inclusion:
Amsterdam's multicultural fabric has been a cornerstone of its identity. The city has historically welcomed immigrants, contributing to its vibrant cultural landscape. This inclusivity has fostered creativity, economic dynamism, and social cohesion. Other cities can learn from Amsterdam's example by actively promoting policies that encourage diversity, ensuring that all voices are heard and valued. This not only enriches the community but also stimulates innovation and problem-solving.

2. Foster Economic Resilience Through Diversification:
Amsterdam's economic evolution illustrates the importance of diversification. From its early trade routes to the establishment of the Dutch East India Company, the city has continually adapted its economic base to changing circumstances. This adaptability has shielded it from economic downturns. Cities facing economic uncertainty should consider developing a diverse portfolio of industries, investing in technology, creative sectors, and green initiatives, thereby reducing reliance on any single economic driver.

3. Prioritize Sustainable Urban Development:
In recent years, Amsterdam has become a leader in sustainability, striving to balance urban growth with environmental stewardship. The city's focus on sustainable transportation, green spaces, and eco-friendly infrastructure has made it a model for urban planning. Other municipalities can learn from Amsterdam's commitment to sustainability, implementing policies that prioritize environmental health while accommodating urban expansion. This

approach not only enhances quality of life but also addresses pressing global challenges like climate change.

4. Support Cultural and Artistic Expression:
The Golden Age of Amsterdam was marked by significant cultural and artistic achievements, including the works of masters like Rembrandt and Vermeer. The city's investment in arts and culture has continued to yield social benefits, fostering a sense of community and identity. Other cities should recognize the importance of supporting the arts, as cultural initiatives can drive tourism, enhance community engagement, and stimulate local economies. Investments in creative spaces and programs can cultivate a lively cultural scene that enriches urban life.

5. Engage in Inclusive Governance and Civic Participation:
Amsterdam has a history of political activism and civic engagement, enabling citizens to influence decision-making processes. This participatory approach has fostered trust between the government and the community. Other cities can benefit from encouraging active citizen participation in governance, creating platforms for dialogue and collaboration. This engagement not only empowers residents but also leads to more responsive and effective policies that reflect the community's needs.

6. Prepare for Globalization:
As a historical trading hub, Amsterdam has navigated the complexities of globalization adeptly. The city's ability to harness global networks while preserving local identity is a valuable lesson. Cities today should cultivate a sense of place while embracing global connections, ensuring that local businesses thrive in the global marketplace. This balance can strengthen local economies and enhance cultural exchanges, contributing to a city's overall vitality.

7. Learn from History:
Finally, Amsterdam's history teaches the importance of reflecting on past experiences to inform future decisions. The city has weathered crises, from wars to economic downturns, often emerging stronger and more united. Other cities should prioritize historical awareness, using lessons from the past to address contemporary challenges, fostering resilience and community spirit.

In conclusion, Amsterdam's historical experiences encapsulate valuable lessons in diversity, economic resilience, sustainability, cultural investment, civic engagement, and the importance of historical reflection. As cities worldwide face complex challenges in an ever-evolving global landscape, these lessons can guide them toward innovative solutions and a more equitable future.

Amsterdam's Global Influence

Amsterdam, the capital city of the Netherlands, has long served as a pivotal hub for cultural, political, and economic activities, exerting a profound influence on global trends. This influence has evolved through its rich history, strategic geographical location, and progressive societal values, positioning Amsterdam as a city that not only reflects the complexities of modern life but also actively shapes them.

Cultural Influence

Amsterdam's cultural impact is perhaps most vividly seen through its artistic legacy. The Dutch Masters, particularly Rembrandt and Vermeer, established a narrative of artistic excellence that resonates well beyond the borders of the Netherlands. The city's museums, such as the Rijksmuseum and the Van Gogh Museum, attract millions of visitors annually, promoting a global appreciation for Dutch art and culture. This cultural significance has also fostered a vibrant contemporary arts scene, where modern artists continue to explore and redefine the boundaries of creativity, thereby influencing global artistic movements.

Moreover, Amsterdam's multicultural environment has enriched its cultural landscape. With a diverse population stemming from various ethnicities and backgrounds, the city has become a melting pot of ideas, traditions, and artistic expressions. Events like the Amsterdam Dance Event and the Amsterdam International Documentary Film Festival showcase global talent and foster cross-cultural collaborations, reinforcing the city's role as a cultural beacon in a globalized world.

Political Influence

Politically, Amsterdam has been a longstanding advocate for democracy, human rights, and social justice. Its historical significance as a center for the Dutch Republic established a foundation for principles that resonate within contemporary global politics. The city has been at the forefront of various social movements, promoting civil rights and progressive policies that have inspired similar movements worldwide.

Amsterdam's role within the European Union (EU) further amplifies its political influence. As a city that embodies the ideals of European integration, it serves as a platform for discussions on policy-making, sustainability, and international cooperation. The presence of numerous international organizations, including the International Criminal Court (ICC) and various environmental initiatives, underscores Amsterdam's commitment to addressing global challenges, positioning it as a crucial player in international relations.

Economic Influence

Economically, Amsterdam has evolved into one of Europe's leading financial centers. The establishment of the Amsterdam Stock Exchange in the 17th century marked a significant milestone in the development of modern finance. Today, the city hosts a plethora of multinational corporations, startups, and innovative tech companies, attracting investment and talent from around the world. This economic dynamism not only contributes to local prosperity but also influences global economic trends, particularly in sectors such as finance, technology, and sustainable development.

Furthermore, Amsterdam's strategic location as a port city has historically facilitated trade and commerce. Its well-established logistics and infrastructure networks have made it a central node in global supply chains. The Port of Amsterdam, one of the largest in Europe, plays a vital role in international shipping, trade, and logistics, enhancing the city's reputation as a global trade hub.

Conclusion

In summary, Amsterdam's global influence is a multifaceted phenomenon shaped by its rich cultural heritage, progressive political ideals, and robust economic framework. The city serves as a model for blending tradition with innovation, advocating for inclusivity while fostering creativity. As Amsterdam continues to navigate the complexities of a rapidly changing world, its historical experiences and ongoing contributions position it as an influential player on the global stage, inspiring cities and societies around the world to embrace cultural diversity, democratic values, and economic innovation. This enduring legacy not only reflects Amsterdam's past but also illuminates the path toward a sustainable and inclusive future.

The Future of Amsterdam

As Amsterdam stands at the threshold of a new era, its dynamic history provides both insights and lessons that can help navigate the challenges and opportunities it faces in the future. The city's evolution from a small fishing village at the mouth of the Amstel River to a global metropolis has been marked by resilience, innovation, and adaptability. These characteristics will be pivotal as Amsterdam confronts contemporary issues such as climate change, social inequality, and rapid globalization.

One of the most pressing challenges on Amsterdam's horizon is climate change. Historically, the city has been adept at managing its water systems, which allowed it to thrive on reclaimed land. However, rising sea levels and increased rainfall threaten this delicate balance. Drawing from its historical experience, Amsterdam has begun to implement sustainable urban planning initiatives, such as green roofs, permeable pavements, and expanded green spaces. The resilience demonstrated during past challenges, such as the rebuilding efforts after World War

II, suggests that the citizens and authorities can collaborate effectively to develop innovative solutions that enhance the city's ecological sustainability.

Social inequality is another challenge that Amsterdam must address moving forward. The city has long been a hub of cultural diversity, but economic disparities have become more pronounced in recent years. The historical context of social movements in Amsterdam, from the labor rights activism of the 19th century to the countercultural revolutions of the 1960s and 70s, illustrates the city's capacity for social reform and activism. Future opportunities for Amsterdam lie in leveraging this spirit of activism to foster inclusive policies that ensure equitable access to resources, housing, and employment. Initiatives focused on multiculturalism and integration will be essential to maintain the city's identity as a tolerant and progressive urban center.

Globalization presents both challenges and opportunities for Amsterdam. The city's historical role as a trading hub established a legacy of international connectivity that can be harnessed in a globalized economy. However, the influx of multinational corporations can also lead to pressures on local businesses and cultural identity. To navigate this, Amsterdam can draw lessons from its past by nurturing local entrepreneurship and promoting sustainable tourism that respects the city's unique character. By balancing global engagement with local interests, Amsterdam has the potential to become a model for other cities facing similar pressures.

Technological innovation is also set to redefine Amsterdam's future. The city's historical embrace of trade and commerce suggests an innate adaptability to new economic realities. The rise of the tech sector and the emergence of Amsterdam as a smart city present opportunities for economic growth and enhanced quality of life. However, the challenge lies in ensuring that technological advancements do not exacerbate existing inequalities. Creating tech policies that prioritize inclusivity and accessibility will be crucial in shaping a future where all residents can benefit from innovation.

Lastly, the spirit of community and citizen activism, deeply embedded in Amsterdam's history, will continue to play a vital role in shaping its future. As the city faces multifaceted challenges, fostering civic engagement and participation will empower residents to contribute to decision-making processes, ensuring that developments reflect the collective needs and aspirations of the community.

In conclusion, as Amsterdam looks to the future, its rich historical tapestry offers valuable lessons. By harnessing the resilience, innovation, and community spirit that have defined its past, Amsterdam can effectively address contemporary challenges while seizing opportunities for sustainable growth and social equity. The way forward will not only reflect the city's history but also shape a vibrant and inclusive future for generations to come.

Printed in Great Britain
by Amazon